D1076885

OUT
OF THE
BLUE

UNFOLD YOUR WINGS AND
SET YOUR SPIRIT FREE

Michael Kemball
A true story about learning to fly

AuthorHouse™ UK Ltd.
500 Avebury Boulevard
Central Milton Keynes, MK9 2BE
www.authorhouse.co.uk
Phone: 08001974150

Cover and layout designed by
Chimera Design Ltd
2 Harlequin Avenue, Brentford
Middlesex TW8 9EW
www.chimeradesign.co.uk
Phone: 020 8569 8994

First published by AuthorHouse 2/1/2010.

ISBN: 978-1-4389-5562-9 (sc)

This book is printed on acid-free paper.

Credits:
Paragliding photograph (Back Cover): Asen Baramov
Flying man lino print: Georgia Kemball
Michael Kemball's photograph (Back Cover): Tim Foster
Text References:
1 Page 95 – The Croatian Survivor, Davor Jardas, www.xcmag.com
(published in Dec-Jan edition) Saturday, 26th July, 1997
2 Page 105 – Debra Fentress: www.debrafentress.com2010

For

Georgia

Contents

Introduction

"Everyone who lives dies;
yet not everyone who dies has lived.
We choose flying not to escape life,
but to prevent life from escaping us!"
www.skynomad.com

Since ancient times flying symbolises freedom, in man's quest to take to the air and let his spirit soar. The symbolism of flight is powerful; there is an energy that resonates within.

The experience of learning to free fly was profound for me. It's something that I hope you encounter in these pages or by learning to fly yourself, if you are inspired to take the leap.

After flying with wild eagles, I wrote down my experience to share with those close to me; the feedback from my family and friends inspired me. It provided the trigger to write this book, integrating the various levels of my experience into the fabric of my story about learning to paraglide.

What is paragliding? It is a form of free flying

without a motor where you glide through the air after leaping from a height, using a wide canopy resembling a parachute or kite, attached by a series of lines to a harness, into which you are strapped.

What I wish to share with you is the experience of learning, together with the sense of awe. There is another dimension – the miraculous transformation within that enables you to reach heights you dream about, physically, emotionally, intellectually and even spiritually.

I learned to fly in the spring of 2006 in Bulgaria in Eastern Europe. My instructors created a special climate in which to learn to fly, including a philosophical perspective that reaches into the mystical and spiritual. Their approach revealed a world of magic and wonder.

Part of my assignment in Bulgaria was the role of a trainer, to guide and develop people. The experience of learning to fly provided an ideal environment to put into practise the methods and techniques that I was teaching. In recent years I have been drawn to various branches of esoteric philosophy; learning to fly provided a fantastic climate in which to experiment with this knowledge, giving immediate and powerful feedback. The gift of flight brings life to abstract principles.

This book is a description of a personal journey, given as a present from a father to his daughter, an act of love. I trust that you accept it in the spirit intended. You can read this book as a story of someone sharing his experience and learning with you, or use it to guide you on an adventure to unfold your wings and reveal your magnificence.

Introduction

These are not only my adventures, as you read you may find that the story triggers experiences of your own. When they resonate within you, notice what you feel inside and pay attention to what you may consider doing differently. What would happen when you make changes in your life? When you experiment, there is a paradox – to get the best result act as if you already know how to do it!

Bulgaria is a beautiful country, a magical land, a hidden gem – a gateway between Europe and the Orient. Its recent history is one of considerable upheaval; it hasn't been easy. The people are kind, hospitable and generous, a mountain nation with a Mediterranean approach to life. Seeing the world through Eastern eyes altered my outlook as their culture adds elegance and depth to the traditional Western approach to dealing with others and certainly enhanced my own life.

This book is a tribute to all the people who extended their warm hands of friendship to me during a time of personal turbulence, as well as teaching me to fly. This is the gift that I wish to pass on to you; it is my way of saying thank you, *'blagodarya'*.

CHAPTER 1

The Call to Fly

*"To discover new lands
one must first consent to lose sight of the shore"*
André Gide

Many people believe that we are not meant to fly. Others believe that we are all angels; it's just that some find it easier to discover their wings. Have you ever wondered what it would be like to fly? Or even wished you could?

Can you remember a time, in your dreams, when you took to the skies? Feeling the wind, that sense of soaring, the air whistling by as you look down from above, on a world far below. You see things from a different perspective high in the heavens.

There is a tug inside, an insistence to look and listen, to wake up. So it remains a dream, unless, of course, you choose to make your dreams come true. To fly or not to fly, the choice is yours!

It was my fiftieth birthday when I became aware

of my calling to fly. It was not long after my father's death and the break up of my marriage. I was at my sister Nico's house in London, when she asked me, "So Mike, what would you *really* like to do?"

"I want to fly," I replied, the words came out of the blue before I realised what I had said. To my amazement, my family and friends took me seriously and their birthday gift was a contribution towards my flying lessons. By accepting the present, I took on the challenge and committed myself to learning to fly.

On water I prefer sailing to using a motor; it's about harnessing the elements. It means tuning in, reading the wind and water, anticipating what is likely to happen next. You make mistakes and so learn the skill and art, until it becomes second nature to you.

There was an appeal in the idea of soaring in the air like a bird. There is a freedom in letting go and living in the moment. I yearned to fly through the heavens, to feel the wind on my face. However, I knew that I didn't want to fly a plane but I also didn't know what type of flying lessons I wanted. So I waited until the time was right to see what would appear.

The months passed. An opportunity arose to work in Bulgaria and I accepted an assignment in Sofia, the capital city. Tony, a friend with whom I had worked previously, had invited me to help him with a major change programme of a formerly state-owned company, which, at that time, had been purchased by a western private equity fund for the first time. It was my first stay in Eastern Europe beyond a fleeting visit.

Old concrete apartment blocks lined the highway into the city from the airport, packed snow and grit formed mounds along the edge of the road when I arrived in mid March. It had an air of scruffiness; the buildings were unkempt and unloved with little of the polish of the west. The writing on the signs was mainly in Cyrillic script, which seemed impenetrable.

The people were friendly although they did not appear to smile much. I did wonder what I was letting myself into, and whether I had made a big mistake.

I threw myself into the assignment, aware that, with the confusion that change creates throughout the organisation, aligning the new and old approaches was stretching the organisation and people to breaking point. I focused on the job that needed to be done, paying scant attention to the human aspect. It took a while for me to realise that I came across as brash and arrogant, insensitive to the concerns and abilities of others. After reluctantly accepting the feedback from Valeriy and Mira with whom I worked, I adjusted my approach, and I began to get a better understanding of the people and their culture.

As I became more deeply involved in the project, I worked more closely with the managers and sales teams around the country. It became apparent on a trip to Varna and Burgas on the Black Sea in June that the results weren't coming through because people didn't really know how to deliver. Mira was my guide and translator. Over long meetings in Varna we teased out the issues and concerns. We agreed action plans and the results followed with dramatic improvements in the following months. Mira and I then set off on car journeys to visit the major towns one-by-one, traversing the length and breadth of the country, across mountains and lush valleys. Our discussions stretched out sometimes late into the night to persuade the key managers to shed their bureaucratic chains. Bulgaria and its people began to open up to me. Gradually, the results began to shine through, together with a feeling of belonging and camaraderie.

In late autumn, I was hiking up high on the majestic mountain, Vitosha, which rises close by the capital. For nearly two hundred years it has served as a nature park for the citizens to escape the confines of the city.

I stopped to rest looking at the view from the mountain while I enjoyed the quiet and solitude. Silently, behind the rocks to my right, a large wing appeared out of the blue and drifted past. It was followed by a red one, then another ... and another.

I stared transfixed, watching the paragliders weave effortlessly round the rocks. I had never seen anything like it before; the impact was like an explosion in my head. "Wow! Imagine being able to fly. Just suppose I could. Now that is what I want to do!"

A little voice inside me started, "No, don't be silly, you can't do that." To which another replied, "Can't you? Why not? Would you like to? What's stopping you?" Something deep inside had locked onto this wonderful form of flying like a magnet, at the same time I grappled with the implications of flight.

Winter set in and the months went by. Over drinks at a birthday celebration in the Sofia office one evening, a small group of us discussed the things we wanted to do in our lives. I mentioned what I had seen on the mountain and my yearning to fly. Dyan, who worked on the same floor as me but with whom I had previously only exchanged pleasantries, replied "Well, I have two friends who paraglide. I have been on a tandem flight with one, Daniel. It was an amazing experience. If you want to learn, look up an organisation called Skynomad on the internet; they're meant to be good."

He scribbled down the name and web address on a scrap of paper. I didn't do anything for a while, but, a few weeks later, after deliberating whether this was really something I wanted to do and having lost his note, I asked him for the details once more. This time I took action.

My assignment in Bulgaria which was originally short-term kept being extended. I had left London and a broken marriage for Eastern Europe, walking away from my old life to lick my wounds and work out what to do.

Before I launched myself into the air, rock bottom beckoned. When I looked in the mirror, I no longer recognised the person who stared back at me. "Who have you become?" I asked. This was not what I had imagined would happen to me. I felt dull, dreary and disconnected; my dreams had faded. I felt that I just didn't want to carry on like this. My old ways were exhausted and it was time to relinquish them.

I contemplated my life and let go. As though

already in flight, I released the person who was no longer me. It was a strange feeling, the experience of letting go. I stared into the void and dropped into the abyss; my wing collapsed and I went into free fall. I waved good-bye to that old me, locked inside his self-made jail; he was swallowed in the darkness of the chasm. It was a parting, the funeral of an old dear friend, and tears rolled down my cheeks.

This 'death' echoed my recent past. Less than three years earlier my father had died. He had lived a full life, sired a large family, an experienced adventurer who travelled widely. His last few months were painful to watch from afar. He became a ghost of the man I remembered as my Dad. I never considered that our relationship was particularly close; it was fraught at times, and he was a formidable force in my life.

That last summer we went to stay with my parents in the paradise they had found together, the old water mill in northern Portugal, which they first fell in love with many years earlier while we still lived in Africa. I knew he was saying good-bye to me, and to each of his children in turn. Although I realised what was happening, it was hard to accept. It was the last night of our stay, he bade me good night and as he mounted the stairs, turned around and fixed me with his now faded, but still piercing, blue eyes. "I'll see you in the morning," he said. It was the last time I saw him alive.

That December, he slipped away in the early morning. My mother was with him at home in the mill. She held his wrist, his pulse getting fainter while she read his letters from when they had first met and married during the Second World War. She had kept all the letters he had written her from the depths of the Burmese jungle behind the Japanese lines.

When she woke up in the early hours that morning, she had a flash of insight; she remembered the letters. She found them and went downstairs to see how he was fairing. She held his hand, and while she read his letters, bringing back memories of almost sixty years earlier, his life quietly faded away.

My sister, Nico, and I arrived in northern Portugal, the night before his funeral. It was late when we crept into the old water mill, which we call home. Everyone had gone to bed and the only signs of life were two black oriental cats, stretched head to tail like Yin and Yang, in front of the dying embers of the fire.

My wife and daughter, Pru and Georgia, had been the first of the family to appear at the Mill. They had come to help look after my father, but he died the day before they arrived. I found them and discovered that they were still awake. Georgia snuggled up to me as we sat on the bed talking in hushed tones. They described how he looked in death as his body was lying in an open casket in the church. I slipped between the sheets and soon fell asleep after my long exhausting journey.

My eyes sprang open before dawn. I could no longer sleep, so I wandered around the mill and garden. I could feel my father's spirit pervade everything around me; he swirled about me, wafting through the leaves, coursing over the weir, flowing through the full river.

Memories of him materialised from behind the camellias and eucalyptus trees – his silly songs making us laugh on the way to school in Luanda; standing on the beach with his nose protected from the sun with aluminium foil; on his boat on the Zambezi River in the stillness of dawn, standing in his shorts, squinting into the early morning sun, his hands on the wheel; the clipped tones of his distinctive voice, his hand on my shoulder, his words of advice.

I could hear him say, "There's a technique to everything" and "You should always leave the table feeling slightly hungry" or explode with, "You must be out of your bloody mind."

As he got older, he often used to say that death was life's greatest adventure. My tears dripped unchecked as the memories pressed in. So what was the real issue? Did I need to confront my own mortality, the knowledge that you can die at any time? Death comes to us all; it's life's greatest adventure. So where are you now?

We arrived early with my mother; Nico and I wanted to pay our respects to him before the small church filled up. I pulled the heavy wooden door slowly open and we stepped inside. Our eyes gradually adjusted to the dim light and we made our way down the aisle, to the wooden coffin in the centre. We stopped and stood; stunned, we stared at his body lying on lace in an open coffin. It was a shell, an old skin left behind when he moved on. It was the first time I had ever just looked at him still and unmoving. In life, he caught you in his eyes and held you; the intensity had electricity, a charge. The spark had now gone; his life force had left his body.

The church filled up with old friends and many villagers. He was well known and respected, the English gentleman. Preciosa, who is all but an adopted daughter to my parents, held a vigil through the night in the church. While we waited for the ritual to begin, my mother pointed out the local characters, including the charmers and scoundrels.

The coffin dominated the centre of the church. Overlooking him was the Virgin Mary with seven swords through her heart, blood weeping from the wounds. The ceremony and ritual slipped into gear and the full Mass began. I sat between my mother and Georgia, who squeezed my hand. On the other side of my mother sat my elder brother, Christopher.

Mass ended. I took up my position at the head of the coffin opposite Christopher, his son Charles behind him. Gomercindo, Preciosa's husband, stood to attention behind me. We lifted the coffin and the priest led the procession to the burial plot. With slow deliberate steps, we carried my father to his resting place. Four men walked together, held by the memory and remains of one man, my father. The symbolism hit deep.

We lowered the coffin. The earth thudded against the wood, each thump hammering home with finality, until Mum said that she could stand the sound no more. She led us out of the churchyard and we walked away.

The days afterwards were intimate, unguarded, as our family bonded while people came and went.

The discussions amongst us six children at first focused on our mother and what she should do next. Should she stay here alone? Where should she go?

Jessica, my eldest sister, worked her magic in the kitchen the evening of the day following the funeral. We sat around the table for dinner, Mum at the head of the table, the Matriarch. She was always the strength behind the throne. She held us all together, in her web. "I'm not leaving. I'm staying here," she announced. "In case any of you have other ideas," she added with a smile. That was the end of that discussion.

It was a time to catch up with each other, to reach out and re-connect. We had long walks on the beach together, in the crisp winter sun, the Atlantic rollers thundered on the rocks. Evenings were spent in the warm glow of a log fire. We shared hopes and disappointments, and underneath we still cared for each other. We connected, death bringing us closer together.

Something curious happened on my last evening. Our sailing boat, which Dad and I had bought many years ago, had been washed downstream two years previously. The boat reappeared, but the mast vanished in the flood. We searched the river down to the sea each summer, looking for the mast – nothing!

That evening, I followed the narrow path along the riverbank used by fishermen. There was a gleam from the middle of the river. A small shaft glinted above the water line and the other end was lodged in the sandy riverbed. I leant over the water, balancing from a branch in one hand, with the other hand I easily withdrew the long aluminium mast out of the river, like Excalibur being drawn out of the rock.

The death and funeral of my father shifted something deep inside me. Until you really acknowledge that you are going to die, you do not feel the pull to be fully who you are. Perhaps his death awakened in me an awareness of my own mortality, or I no longer needed his approval at an unconscious level, permitting a more authentic me to be revealed.

My earliest memory of flying was as a young boy of eight. I'm the fourth in a family of six children, three girls and three boys and grew up in Africa, in the Portuguese speaking countries of Angola and Mozambique, south of the equator.

A handsome couple, my parents met in the Far East during World War II. My mother was a Wren, from the Women's Royal Naval Service. My father used to tease her that the fourth time they met was at the church altar rails for their wedding in Ceylon.

Shortly afterwards he went to Burma on a secret mission for the British special operations Force 136, operating behind Japanese lines. He was an explosives expert, known as 'Jeep', who led two other British agents and a group of local Burmese to successfully disrupt the Japanese war effort. After the war they lived in Penang and Singapore, where I was born and where we lived until I was three.

Through a quirk of fate, at the time of Malaysian independence, we moved to Luanda in Angola where my father managed a vehicle import business. In those days of the late 1950's Luanda was a cultural melting pot of Africa and Southern Europe, an exotic city on the South Atlantic Ocean, with an elegant waterfront. I still vividly remember the colourfully dressed women on the sides of the streets in the city, where they would sell oranges from large white enamel bowls balanced on their heads, chanting, "Laranja, laranja, laranja", the Portuguese for orange.

As children, we lived in a tropical paradise with a free and easy lifestyle. We went to the English School of Luanda, a relaxed place with no uniform and plenty of games; the other children were mainly American, whose parents were in the oil business. After school in the morning, we spent long afternoons playing on the beach and swimming in the sea.

In 1963 we uprooted ourselves and made the journey across Africa from west to east. From Luanda, Angola on the Atlantic we moved to our new home in Mozambique, another Portuguese colony on the opposite side of Africa on the Indian Ocean, facing the island of Madagascar. We four younger children went with my parents, while the two eldest, Christopher and Jessica, stayed at boarding school. We climbed aboard the Portuguese cargo ship on the first leg of our voyage and watched Luanda disappear behind us on the horizon as we headed out into the South Atlantic. We followed the coast, and pulled into the southern Angolan port of Mossamedes, a dry town in a harsh empty desert that seemed far away from the lush tropics of Luanda. We travelled south along the skeleton coast of Namibia until we reached the Cape of Good Hope.

There was a Portuguese family on the ship, but we were the only foreigners. Ros, my elder sister, at ten years old was the eldest and the gentlest of our tribe of four. I was next, followed by my sister, Nico, and my younger brother Benj, aged five. We spent the days in the small swimming pool or playing games, occasionally interrupted by sightings of flying fish, dolphins and whales. Like the Portuguese seafarers of old, we sighted land again at the southern tip of Africa. Arriving at the port of Cape Town in the evening after dark, the lights twinkled all around the bay, an enormous amphitheatre, with a canopy of stars above. The sense of adventure was tangible.

We climbed into the American Ford we had brought with us on the ship from Angola; the Thunderbird was all wings and chrome, with a gear stick on the steering column. From the Cape, my parents took turns driving, while we kids spread ourselves on the single long back seat, watching the scenery roll by along the Garden Coast, through South Africa, into the high interior to Southern Rhodesia, now Zimbabwe.

It was a long drive with little traffic; the road was mostly a strip of tarmac, tracing its way through vast open spaces. During the long sections we got bored and exasperated my parents from our seat in the back. The scenery was spectacular, although we were too young to appreciate the images that flashed by.

We made stops on the way, a welcome relief from long days in the car. We stayed with Gavin, an old friend of Mum's, who lived in an old rambling house on a sugar estate in Natal. Ros, in great pain, was hospitalised with appendicitis, so we had the luxury of a week in a hotel in Pietermaritzburg in Natal until she was discharged. We stayed at the Kruger National Park; I watched mesmerized as the lions lazily ate their prey on a hill in the heat of the midday sun.

In Zimbabwe Benj poked a monkey with his finger, which promptly returned the favour by biting him. He was rushed to hospital and had his finger stitched up. Our party now had two invalids. We saw Jessica again when she was released from boarding school to be reunited with our family for a day.

From the cool mountains in the Eastern Highlands of Zimbabwe, we crossed into the tropics of Mozambique, down to the flat lands on the Indian Ocean, to the town of Beira. It was hot, sticky and chaotic and the strong exotic smells reminded me of Angola.

The real high point was the anticipation of my first experience of flying, the final leg of our journey north of Beira. I woke up early that morning in the excitement of catching the plane to our new home in Luabo, a sugar estate on the banks of the Zambezi River, on the coastal plains at the beginning of the delta, where the river emptied into the sea.

On a hot sticky day after an endless wait at the air terminal, we squeezed into the small plane, a six-seater air taxi with a Portuguese pilot, wearing aviator sunglasses and a moustache – a cool Latin version of Biggles!

We taxied along the small airport, the sound of

the engine drowned out any conversation. We waited for clearance to leave; a garbled voice finally crackled noisily over the radio. The pilot opened the throttle and the plane roared down the runway until the pilot pulled the plane up into the sky. We were airborne!

I kept my face pressed to the window as we left the town, all signs of civilization dissolved behind us. We flew over the virgin grasslands of Africa, large herds of buffalo and antelope dotted the savannah below. In order for us to get a better look, the pilot flew low over some of the animals, which scattered as we swooped over them.

We came across a herd of elephants, and as we dived down low, the bulls with large tusks turned around to face us. They were majestic and fearsome, flapping their ears as they charged. The raw wilderness of Africa confronted me; I found it both intimidating and exhilarating at the same time, a voyage into the unknown.

For over an hour and a half we continued across the open expanse of bushland, unspoilt by any sign of civilisation, it spread out beneath us, flat and immense, until the large brown artery of the Zambezi appeared on the horizon, at the end of its journey across the continent to the sea. The pilot shouted above the noise of the engines, this was Luabo.

White houses on stilts clustered by the riverbank, fields of sugar cane spread out to the horizon on the far side of the broad river. The small community seemed so isolated and insignificant perched on the edge of this great river in the vastness of Africa. Was this to be my new home, in the middle of nowhere?

Along the river was a high bank of earth, a dyke to contain the floodwaters, called a murrambala, named after the hills near Sena much further up river from the flatlands. The plane banked over the large sandbanks as we crossed the wide expanse of water.

The runway was a grass landing strip running parallel to the river; it doubled as part of the golf course, a cushion between the houses and the sugar cane. A road ran along the edge of the murrambala to an open hut on the edge of the airstrip. We came down low over the houses, over the grass alongside the road.

The engines got louder; the turbulence near the ground made the plane bounce in all directions. My guts tightened; I took a sharp intake of breath as I braced myself for the landing, hanging on tightly to my seat until my fingers hurt. The plane hit the ground and veered down the grass runway with a roar of engines.

We looked round and smiled at each other with a sense of relief; we were still alive. We'd made it; we'd arrived at last. We squeezed out of the cramped cabin one by one, stepping off the plane's wing, happy to breathe fresh air and stand on the solid earth.

A welcoming committee awaited us. Benj and I ducked and weaved, trying to avoid being smothered by the Portuguese wives, with their large bosoms squeezed into bras shaped like torpedoes, or having my cheek squeezed between thumb and forefinger while they shrieked 'coitadinho'. Eventually we piled into a Land Rover to follow the dirt road, reaching a white house on two storeys with a broad veranda on both floors. We entered a new world on the banks of the Zambezi, our home for many years to come.

This flight became a regular trip. It bridged my two new worlds of school and home, between terms and holidays. I didn't find it easy to reconcile the cold austerity of a Jesuit boarding school with the warmth of a large family. The efficiency of the British colony of Rhodesia differed from the relaxed way of life in Mozambique, an easygoing blend of Portuguese and African attitudes. The crisp cleanliness of the cool dry highlands contrasted with the tropics, where your senses were assaulted and the food was exotic.

Growing up by the great river in the wilds of Africa I was immersed in a world where the smells, the sounds, the colours had an intensity and rawness that made boarding school and city life pale and bland in comparison. Seen through the eyes of a young boy, the energy was awesome!

It was a different reality, a world that danced to a different rhythm. The forces of nature were powerful and untamed. The elements of earth, water, fire, air and spirit were vibrant and visceral. Their potency was latent; like crocodiles and hippos, they lurked below the surface, ever present.

The cyclones pulled up trees like weeds as the air vented its power and substance, unleashing its strength. The Zambezi pulsated with a vitality of its own, teaming with life, as it meandered towards the Indian Ocean. The river had a magnetic pull, drawing all forms of life to it.

The sticky heat of the midday sun brought life to a lethargic halt. The suspense was palpable before the rain came; huge fat warm drops pounded the ground. The clouds passed, the sun reappeared and the heady smell of the earth exploded into the air, filling your lungs.

People walked hand in hand, barefoot on the bare earth, all smiles and laughter. The insects were absorbed in frenzied activity, termites laboured in colossal anthills and elephants wandered down to the opposite bank of the great river, washing and drinking lazily in the warmth of a late afternoon.

As the sun glided over the horizon, the skies were set aflame in a riot of colour. Activity slowed, and then stopped. The creatures of the earth gazed up in wonder. Darkness closed in and the spell broke as the calls of cicadas filled the air. The background sound of drumming throbbed in the distance, the ominous heartbeat of Africa.

The storyteller wove his tale round the glowing coals of the evening fire, shiny faces listened intently, entranced. Groans and laughter were teased from his wide-eyed audience. The stars came out in splendour and the magnificence of the heavens was revealed, your eyes and spirit drawn up in rapture.

Old Joe had travelled everywhere in Africa, from Cairo to Cape Town, East and West. Nobody new how old he was. Long, tall and thin with grizzled hair over a beaming smile and large expressive eyes, he was the only African who spoke a few words of English, picked up on his many travels. He looked after the laundry. After washing the clothes and hanging them up to dry, from six o'clock in the morning he would sit cross-legged in the back yard with his audience arranged around the smouldering fire, sometimes two or three deep.

People would come from far and wide at all times of the day and night to listen to his stories from all over Africa and beyond. As he led his audience into his tale, the drone of his voice would mesmerize you, and we were drawn into his magical world of wonder.

In the late afternoon he would gather the dry clothes in the ironing room, on the ground floor where the stilts held the house above him. Smoke from the hot coals wafted out of the sides of the old iron as he pressed the clothes perfectly, chatting away to us all the time. We followed him back out to the glow of the fire, where he resumed his stories as day faded into night.

I felt that I alternated between two separate worlds of school and home, living two different lives; I plunged from one world to the other, oblivious of one when in the other. The next transition was when I left home at the age of eighteen, this time leaving Africa behind me.

I had been planning to attend university in South Africa, when my father took me aside on my last school holiday, "You should leave. You belong to the wrong generation for Africa; you won't be wanted here. If you do stay, you are committing yourself to a life of disappointment and heartbreak. Go west, go to Europe or America, get out." When I protested, he repeated more forcefully this time, "Listen carefully, get the hell out of Africa!" So I took his advice, left Africa and went to university in England. I went on to business school, joining the corporate world. I travelled and lived in a number of European countries. Pru and I met in Winchester and married in the 1980's; our daughter, Georgia, was born a few years later.

Africa became a world I had left behind, a world that very few seemed to know or care about. When I talked about my old life on the vast continent, others seemed to find it too foreign, and difficult to relate to that alien world. Africa rapidly slid into the recesses of my memory, but at a deeply unconscious level it has always remained engrained in me, the Zambezi is in my blood!

Although I adapted to life in Europe and enjoyed the lifestyle, I never felt that I truly belonged; somehow I was different and sensed I was not being true to myself. There was an inner emptiness, something was missing at a deep level in my life, an aspect of living; it was submersed beneath my awareness which I couldn't express. It finally dawned on me that what I missed was the sense of freedom in the vast space, wilderness and heat, combined with a sense of the exotic.

After the thrill of my first experience of flying to Luabo, as I grew older I flew so often between school and home that it became as commonplace as riding a bus. I still loved the journeys, and never imagined that one-day, many years later, I would learn to soar through the air, master of my own flight.

I have discovered that many people fly in their

dreams – it may be a call for freedom. When you fly in your dreams, you're opening a window to new possibilities, where you can release your soul and set your spirit free. Now this could be exciting!

In the months after my father's death, flying experiences emerged in my dreams, in meditation. There was one dream that recurred, and it resonated deeply within me:

I found myself rising up; I was flying, gazing through the eyes of an eagle, way up in the air. I soared on the wind, wings outstretched, touching the sky, seeing the world from above.

High up in the Andes in Peru, a condor glided below, the white wing marks betrayed his identity. Soaring mountains flanked him and down in the valley flowed the Urubamba River. It was an image from the Incan trail to Machu Picchu, at a time when there were very few travellers, a memorable trip across South America twenty-four years earlier with John, otherwise known as Squatter, a friend from university,

I gazed down on the stone paths of the ancient Incans, tracing their way along the top of the mountain ridge; the world below became smaller as I went higher. Up I soared, higher and higher, drawn to an opening in the sky and the light beyond. I flew up, passing into the light until I was completely enveloped in white light.

I looked around, everything seemed different and yet, at the same time, familiar; the sky glowed in an altered reality. A sailing boat glided across a still, vast expanse of water. Ripples floated out from the boat, radiating in concentric circles. I swooped gracefully out of the sky, landed gently on the very top of the mast, where I found my present. I waited there for a moment before silently spreading my wings once more, launching into the air and soaring way up into the heavens.

The brilliance from the present within cleansed my whole body as the light spread out from within me, radiating outwards until the whole planet, Mother Earth, was bathed in light and I felt her heart beat resonate through me. The waves of light continued to expand to the other planets, Mars, Venus and Mercury, until they reached our star and combined with the rays of the Sun. On went the light to encompass our solar system, through the Milky Way, across the universe, beyond time and space. There was a sense of being an integral part of this magnificence, as a wave is to the ocean. I was in the light and the light was in me.

Flying dreams encourage you to delve deep into your soul and ponder the higher purpose of your life. What are the lessons you need to learn? Are you living enough? Do you love enough? How grateful are you for what you have received on your journey so far?

At the point where we began this tale, the Grim Reaper had entered my life, exposing and annihilating the clutter of my old existence. It created space, allowing change to begin, so that I could begin anew. One of the changes in my life was that Pru and I had decided to separate; it was time to move on. I left for the East, to the Balkans, and my old life began to fall away.

There was a pause, an air of stillness settled over me. It was a time to re-evaluate and I reflected on my circumstances:

"What do you do next? It is up to you to take responsibility for your own life, to deal with whatever comes up. It is up to you to create what you want, and to hang on to what you wish to keep.

Your universe can arrange itself to make your dreams come true, so be careful for what you wish, and to what you pay attention, you may just make them happen! Be sure of your intentions, that they are what you desire - then spread your wings and let your spirit soar."

It was time for a new beginning, a time to take flight.

CHAPTER 2

The Way to Sopot

"When the student is ready, the teacher appears."
Anonymous

Calm and rested, I felt myself waking up. Gentle feelings of curiosity and anticipation drifted into my consciousness. Also apprehension, I have to admit. The air was heavy and cool, and from the sounds outside it had been raining. I could hear tyres rolling across wet cobbles. Metal screeched on metal as the trams laboured past my window. From my bed, I screwed up my eyes to peep through the blinds, a grey mass of cloud lurked behind the window. It was the first day of a long weekend at the end of April in Sofia as Monday was Labour Day.

Today I was hoping to fly. It had been a few months since I had seen those wings fly by on the mountain of Vitosha on the southern edge of Sofia. After checking out Skynomad's website to see what was on offer, I got in touch with them, starting an email correspondence with a guy called Niki. After a week of deliberation, I took the plunge. I decided to enter the world of free flight on a tandem, where you fly with an experienced instructor, strapped to the same wing. I called up Niki to make arrangements.

I had wanted to fly from Vitosha because that was where I had first been captivated by the idea of paragliding. It was also close, and by now familiar, seemingly the perfect place to start. When I asked why he wouldn't do the tandem off Vitosha, Niki replied, "Sopot is better. It's special, you'll see".

As I became better acquainted with Bulgaria, I discovered that Sopot was at the heart of the country in many ways – its geography, its history and its literature. Off the beaten track for foreign tourists, it was about two hours drive, travelling east from Sofia. Niki had arranged for his brother to give me a lift in his car from the square by my apartment. I barely knew where we were going and wasn't sure what I had let myself into but, on a long weekend in spring, it seemed like a good idea!

With limited time to get ready, I jumped out of bed and scrambled into my clothes in a rush; Niki's brother was due at eight. Following the instructions from the website, I put on my 'high, fixing the ankle, boots'.

After locking up the apartment, I walked down the stairs into the morning air. Standing with my overnight bag in the square below with a sense of mounting anticipation, I looked for a yellow Fiesta.

I kept glancing at the time, but it only made it creep by more slowly. I watched the world roll by –

an old pensioner shuffled past the trams and a group of pretty girls were laughing as they crossed the road.

Finally, a battered Fiesta pulled up with two men inside. Was one Niki's brother? I hadn't even met Niki, so how would I know what his brother looked like? I walked over and greeted the driver, "Zdrasti", one of the few words I had learnt.

He replied and I shifted to English, relieved when he appeared to understand. He told me that he was indeed Niki's brother; his name was Miti. The man in the front climbed into the back to make space for me. I jumped in clasping my bag, shaking hands and exchanging names. We had made contact and were on our way!

"Do you fly?" I asked as an opener.

"No", said Miti. The conversation limped along from there and, finally, petered out.

We stopped outside an apartment block. Before disappearing, Miti explained that we were collecting his wife and small child. Together with the other passenger, Plamen, they squeezed into the back of the small car. "No, no, you should stay in the front", Miti insisted when I suggested swapping places with someone in the back.

I was offered a coffee. When Miti handed me the strong coffee in a clear plastic cup, his face lit up as he gave me a gentle shy smile.

We left the city behind us and headed out on the open road. Miti's mobile rang. It was Niki. He handed me the phone.

"The weather is not looking good for today," said

the voice at the other end of the phone. "Do you still want to come? It may change. We probably won't fly. You are welcome to come anyway and see what happens". Miti gave me a choice: I could continue to Sopot or go back to Sofia. It was not a problem to take me back to town, as we hadn't gone that far.

"Well, I haven't got much else to do," I thought. "What the hell? It might clear up. Who knows? I'll go anyway". I told him that I'd continue despite the odds against me. The disappointment showed in my voice.

"You have to be patient if you want to fly," Miti consoled me. We started chatting, the others joined in and then the conversation drifted into Bulgarian.

We passed through lush green valleys, mountains rose on either side as we wound our way through unspoilt forests. As the scenery rolled by, the beauty of the country struck me, despite the grey day. We followed the contour of a long mountain range stretching into the distance to the east, the Stara Planina. We entered the Valley of the Roses over a mountain pass and drove through some scruffy villages. The farmers and gypsies kept to the side of the road in their horse drawn carts as the cars whizzed past.

We reached Sopot and found our way up an old cobbled street to an open square with a white church tower and a water fountain. We pulled up outside a large dark wooden door with 'Skynomad' written above in large letters made of a lighter wood.

Niki ambled over, tall and slim with short dark hair, a shy smile and playful dark eyes. He greeted me in English and we shook hands, "You want to do a tandem flight, do you? Hang around for a while. Let's see. You may get a flight, but you probably will not fly today, maybe tomorrow." He paused, looked me in the eye, and said with a laugh, "Mañana" – it was his favourite word.

He invited me into the club and opened the door. I stepped through to find clusters of people hanging around the courtyard, laughing and chatting, mainly in English.

James struck up a conversation. He was leaving that day, back to the UK. He had long straight brown hair past his shoulders. "Have you flown before? You're doing a tandem flight? You want to learn to fly, do you? It's amazing, fantastic." He offered me his tobacco for a roll-up. We lit up. "You're a natural," he assured me, "I can tell". I smiled, not knowing whether to believe him, but wanting to.

I hung out at the club for a while, wondering what was going on. James mentioned that due to the weather there would be no flying and that some people were going for a barbecue later, up to Beklemeto, an alternative launch site. The courtyard slowly emptied.

We wandered over to a house nearby and James introduced me to the owner, Marcus, a large Brit who worked on the rigs. We stepped over some uprooted floorboards in the main room; he was in the process of doing up the house, which he had recently bought. He handed me a large whisky then proceeded to describe, in detail, some of the terrible accidents that could happen to pilots in paragliders. He leant over his computer to show me video clips from the internet of a guy doing aerobatics, going over the top of the wing, dropping into it and then plummeting into a lake.

My heart sank as I considered what I was doing. He looked up with a big smile, "I'm not putting you off, am I?" He explained that some people could be too casual for their own good and underestimated the risks involved. He was on a mission to make this clear to beginners like me. He started to fly by buying a wing on EBay and began to teach himself in the west of Scotland. After a few scares he decided to find an instructor. He believed that he was lucky to have come out unscathed.

James explained it to me more clearly, "Some people try going it alone and make all the mistakes on their own, then try to work out what to do. This approach does not necessarily result in your learning to fly and significantly reduces your chance of survival!

"Alternatively, you can learn the technique of flying from an instructor in a safe climate. This way you develop your skills in an environment that helps you grow, with other students who help you to maintain your energy and direction. The support counter-balances the pain and disillusion, when your limitations are revealed."

Marcus's young twin boys came over, demanding attention from both of us. Marcus introduced me to Orlin, a great bear of a man with large warm brown eyes, an old scar running down from the left corner of his mouth. Orlin was one of the instructors, he told me. Orlin rolled a cigarette and the conversation flowed, finding its own course. Eventually, we drifted back to the club, stopping for a bite to eat at a small restaurant along the way.

Niki had organised the barbecue trip to one of the alternative launch sites, Beklemeto. The site needed to be cleared of low bushes and scrub, removing anything that could snag the lines at launch. The courtyard filled up again as different people joined the party of Bulgarians, foreigners, pilots, friends and even children.

A small convoy of cars headed up the Stara Planina mountain range. After a series of treacherous turns towards the top, we pulled off the road, down a dirt track and onto a grass clearing, the launch site of Beklemeto.

A cold mist surrounded us. Groups of people were hanging around; a few started to hack away at different plants and I asked a grey-haired guy what I could do to help. He invited me to help him uproot the remains of a flat bush. The two of us dug at a stump, chatting while we worked. He was from the Peace Corps and based three hours drive away with a group of Americans. Every few weeks he joined the pilots in Sopot for a weekend break from the people with whom he lived and worked. He had learnt to fly in North America and decided to pick it up again while in Bulgaria.

A large plastic bottle of beer was passed around the mixed bunch of Bulgarians and foreigners, held together by a common thread, an interest in flying. A large branch for the barbecue was dragged across the grass clearing. The mist closed in and the work petered out. My new friend reckoned that I would be very lucky to get a flight; there was almost no chance of flying.

Everyone gravitated towards the heat of the fire where chicken and sausages were cooking over hot coals. As soon as the food was ready, we tucked in, hungry after the hard manual work. We relaxed and warmed up from the damp chill as the beer flowed and the banter escalated. Having long since given up hope of a flight that day and resting in the warm company, I helped myself to more.

Niki walked up to me. "Do you still want to fly? Are you ready?" he asked, "We're going, now." Taken by surprise, I stopped, and then followed him over to where all the equipment was laid out on the grass. We had to move quickly if we wanted to catch the opportunity of an opening in the cloud to the valley below. My heart lifted and my guts tightened.

Somebody helped me to fasten the harness and helmet; all the straps and buckles were confusing. My breath quickened in apprehension. The canopy, or wing, was stretched behind us. Niki cleared the lines. It looked so flimsy - and how on earth did it fly?

My harness was strapped to Niki's, which in turn was connected to the wing; I stood in front of him. "When we go, keep running, even when your feet leave the ground. I will tell you when to stop." My heart pounded, my knees felt weak.

For a moment I wondered if I had lost my mind. With my heart in my throat, a sense of anguish began to rise up inside me. Here I was in the middle of nowhere, throwing myself off a misty mountain in a leap of faith with a complete stranger, attached by string to a sheet of flimsy fabric lying on the grass; and all I had to do was to suspend my disbelief and keep running! Was I a complete fool? It felt surreal.

I took a deep breath to calm myself, staring ahead into the dark hole in the white mist.

"GO!" yelled Niki behind me. I forced my feet in front of me, leaning forward as instructed. The huge canopy lifted off the ground behind us; I couldn't see it as I pressed forward but could feel the strong pull through the shoulder straps of my harness. We strode down the mountain almost tripping over each other's feet.

Everything seemed to happen in slow motion. The harness hoisted me up and we were airborne. All of a sudden everything was smooth and effortless; the transition was instantaneous. My feet lifted off the ground, still peddling. We scraped across the grass and then over the tops of the trees and into the mist; the ground below disappeared. "You can stop running now," said the voice behind me with a smile.

We dived into a hole in the bank of cloud. All around the pale milky light cocooned us as we floated through a sea of white. We came out the other side and suddenly the whole valley was spread out below – it was breathtaking with the mountains of Sredna Gora rising up in the distance. I was breathless, spellbound and suspended in space. It felt like a dream, one minute I was having a barbecue on the side of a mountain and the next I was floating through space.

We glided smoothly and effortlessly and I could hear the sound of dogs barking below mingled with the wind whistling through the lines. There was nothing in front or below me; my eyes followed the lines from the harness to the wing above, to see what was holding me up. Niki handed me the two controls, one for each hand. "Pull down on one side", he said calmly. I pulled tentatively with my left hand. We slowly banked away from the mountain. Then with my right, we turned the other way. We floated down gently under the force of gravity, still high above the ground.

Niki took back the controls. He pulled hard on the right, shifting his weight simultaneously. We spun round to the right, leaving my guts behind. The centrifugal force strangled my breath. Then we did the same to the left. I caught my breath as we levelled out.

"Can you see the ruins over there?" he gestured. I stared below at the ground. The foundations of a large building became visible, etched into the grass. A herd of goats in shades of brown, from white to black, were dotted on a sea of green. We glided effortlessly through space and time, looking down on the world below.

As we drifted towards the earth the valley came closer and closer. "When we land, keep running. And keep your knees bent," he instructed.

We came down to land, aiming at the centre of an open expanse of wild meadow. It seemed a bit hit and miss; I braced myself for the shock, wondering what was going to happen. The ground rushed up to meet us. Niki braked by pushing down hard on both controls. We slowed, lifted slightly and then touched down. My feet hit the ground, and the harness pulled me back. We landed safely, slowing rapidly to a halt as the wing dropped neatly behind us.

Lost in the silence of the moment, we both stood in the middle of the field; everything stopped. For an instant, it felt strange to feel the force of gravity and have the earth pushing up against my feet. A rush charged through my whole body, a vibrant sensation, leaving an inner glow in its trail. Niki gave me a huge smile; I beamed back at him and I couldn't thank him enough.

In a daze I climbed out of the gear. We folded the wing and packed everything into a large rucksack, which Niki threw onto his back. We walked across the field to the road, and then a mile or so to the main highway. On the way he told me stories about some of his cross-country flights. The time flew by, before long we were standing on the roadside hitching a lift back to Sopot; he told a good tale.

I could hardly believe that I'd just flown; it seemed to go so quickly – and yet the feeling of floating seemed timeless. The world around me had changed; it felt different, sounded different, looked different, and even smelt different. My heart was racing; I was on a high.

A black car pulled up. A middle-aged man offered us a lift and we climbed in. Niki and the driver chatted away in Bulgarian in the front. Sitting in the back I contemplated how I had reached this point in my life, my transition during the day and what I had learnt:

After a time of deliberation, you make the decision to take the plunge; only you can make that decision, no one else can do that for you. When you start on your journey, hold on to your dream; be firm and hang in there, circumstances will appear to test you. Allow situations to unfold and develop, let go of the form. The characters and lessons will appear in your life, when you allow them to materialise. When you take the plunge, face your fear and push through, remember that fear is a veil in front of the entrance to a whole new world that awaits you. Keep moving forward.

I reran the experience again and again through my mind. I knew I was hooked. I swallowed it whole. This was it. I was going on the beginner's course tomorrow, I was ready to fly.

CHAPTER 3

Learning to Fly

"There is an art to flying.
The knack lies in learning how to
throw yourself at the ground and miss."
Douglas Adams

The morning sun shone into the courtyard of the clubhouse. The atmosphere was relaxed as a group of pilots hung out together, chatting, waiting for the right conditions. It was an open house and there was plenty of time. I slipped back into an easy style of living that seemed familiar, an approach I abandoned a long time ago. It was like putting on a favourite item of clothing, it felt right.

Niki appeared at the door and asked me how much I weighed. He chucked me a bag with a wing in it, "You'll need a harness too," he added. In order to check some of the fittings, someone helped me to strap the harness up to a weird contraption of wooden struts held by ropes hanging in mid air from a rafter.

I climbed into the harness and tried to put it on, fumbling ineffectually with the straps. "Let me show you," explained Zabdi, a Scottish instructor from the Isle of Arran who was checking out Bulgaria with a group of students. "You need to learn how to put this on by rote, because you must remember every step. You're talking about your life".

She recited a litany. "Leg straps, chest strap, helmet, karabiners ..." she paused. "If you don't remember your leg straps, you could have a problem after take off ... sliding through the harness and then what?" she added with a grin.

The karabiners are the metal clips that attach the two sides of the harness to some straps – the risers, which in turn are connected by numerous lines to the wing. I tried on the leg straps, wrestling with the buckle.

When I finally clipped them on, I was told to pull hard on the leg straps to ensure they had clicked into the buckle – sand and grit could cause them not to catch. I fastened the chest strap, which went across my hips when I stood up, and wondered why it was called a chest strap.

Then the helmet went on; it was bright pink, obviously not a favourite with the other pilots. It must have been on special offer when it was bought. "I'm glad it's you who's got that helmet today and not me. You know you look a complete prat," teased one of the student pilots.

Zabdi pulled and tugged on various straps. I felt trapped and caught, trussed up like a chicken. "How the hell can you fly like this?" I wondered.   More advice poured in from others and I felt overloaded with information. Would I ever remember it all?

The courtyard emptied. The cars outside took the students to the chairlift, which carried them from the base to the top of the mountain. Niki led me into the office. "For theory," he clarified "and then we'll go to the training hill."

We sat down at a low coffee table. He explained how the wing flew when it was inflated, with diagrams of airflows. How you were suspended by different rows of lines. How you could use the control lines (at the trailing edge) to steer and slow down. How the wing flew at a constant speed through the air, depending on the angle of attack. The difference between airspeed and groundspeed was determined by your direction relative to the wind. We moved on to wind flows around large objects like mountains, trees and houses. Followed by turbulence, rotors and down winds, the positions and situations in which you never want to find yourself and their consequences. I was learning a whole new language, together with a different way to see and interpret the world.

He was patient in answering me and when there were no more questions left, we tidied up and entered the courtyard. "Grab your stuff and come with me," Niki said as he wandered onto the cobbled street. I wrestled with the large backpack that contained everything I needed to fly. I felt the pride of the novice combined with an inner conviction that I was entering a whole new dimension, the world of flight. I felt full of high expectations and ready to take my first steps along the path that leads to the sky. The innocent stepped forth.

I strapped my bag onto the roof rack of a hand-painted car. It was a Moskvich, which is an old Russian car, and this specimen must have been at least 20 years old, in a colourful primary green. There were large dents on the bonnet, which had been used as a seat. Synthetic tufted orange covers were held on to the chair by elastic. There was a hole in the dashboard for a radio, wires dangled loosely behind. After a few attempts to start the engine, the old beast leapt into life. With a grinding of gears, we lurched down the cobbled street, past the restaurant where we had eaten only the day before.

We joked about the old car and Niki recounted how he started paragliding many years previously. He began with mountaineering, which he learnt as a boy. His father was a mountain guide and taught him the ways of the mountain. He loved the idea of leaping off the summit and gliding to the bottom, instead of hiking all the way down. He described the old wings, barely different from an old parachute, in a square design. "It's moved on a long way since those early days," he reassured me.

We left the main road. Walnut trees lined either side of the lane. Vineyards and fields of roses lay beyond. This was the Valley of the Roses, the source of much of the world's rose oil, for perfume.

"So, do you value your life?" he asked casually, turning slowly to look me in the eye. He caught me by surprise. "Now that's a good question," I thought. "Did I value my life?" I observed my mind begin to wander off at a tangent as I contemplated the implications of his question.

"Yes," I assured him, "I do value my life."

"Good," he continued, "Because we need to make sure you follow the routine for launch and landing, every time. You need to learn it off by heart so that you do it without thinking. It should save your life."

We followed a dirt road with large potholes, over a railway line towards the training hill. To the right in the distance there was a large graveyard "for those that didn't make it through the training!' Niki remarked with a straight face. We parked under a tree at the base of a hill, around forty metres high, surrounded by ploughed fields. We were in the middle of a large flat valley. There was a patch of grass at the base of the hill; to my left by the road were trellises with vines growing roses in between. Barbed wire connected the concrete posts at chest height. Some large holes had been gouged out of the hill above the vineyard.

We spread the wing on the grass at the base of the hill. Niki showed me the vents and lines. He pointed out what he had explained to me with diagrams in our earlier theory session. Holding the risers, he tossed the wing gracefully into the air, steadied it in the gentle breeze, and controlled it with a small tweak on a line now and again. He held it there, with no effort; he was in full control, the master. It looked so easy.

He explained how to do a forward take off by holding the 'A risers' – the straps that connect to the lines at the leading edge, the front of the canopy. "You run forward, the wing rises up from behind you. When it is above you, pull down on the control lines, they connect to the trailing edge, at the rear of the canopy, then you run."

I struggled into the harness and clipped on the pink helmet. Niki attached the risers to the karabiners. "Off you go," he said. I took a few steps forward into the light wind. Up went the canopy. It pitched forcefully to the right, wrenching and dragging me into the field with a life of its own, while I tried, ineffectually, to control it. The wretched thing tied itself into a knot of fabric and lines.

Niki extricated me. He patiently explained what to do differently next time. I repeated the launch with several more attempts until I managed to station the wing above me, briefly, before it threw me around again, like a cat playing with a mouse.

To launch, there are three distinct steps, which are simple in theory:

Step 1: Inflation

Step 2: Control

Step 3: Accelerate

Inflation is where you lift the wing up into the wind from behind you. The cells of the wing inflate with air, creating the aerofoil shape that allows the wing to fly. The canopy acts like a sail, the wind pins you back as it lifts off the ground, until the wing shoots above your head.

At this point you slow it, by pulling on the control lines, which brake the wing to hold it above you, to stop it overshooting and collapsing in a heap in front of you. This is the second step 'control'. If you pause, it loses momentum and collapses. So you have to move quickly to the next step – accelerate –

which means, 'run like hell and don't stop till well after you leave the ground'.

We moved to the base of the hill. I repeated the launch process, moving slowly up the hill after each two or three attempts. I gradually learned new skills with each step. Niki showed me how to make a 'rose' with the wing by gathering all the lines together, close to the canopy. It radiated into a voluminous flower of purple and red. I tossed it over my shoulder as Niki demonstrated to me, making it easier to walk up the hill. I felt like a debutante in a ball gown; the fabric rustled with every movement I made.

Before each attempt, I went through the ritual pre-flight check: leg straps, chest strap, helmet strap, karabiners, 'A' lines clear, leading edge, air space clear to left and right, wind speed and direction. It became a mantra that I could recite in my sleep. With each attempt I ran further down the hill. Gravity persisted in holding me firmly in its grasp, despite my attempts to break free.

The sun beat down. Progress was slow and painful. I was hot, sticky and tired. My consolation was the heady aroma of wild herbs and camomile, crushed by my boots as I trudged agonizingly up the hill.

There were so many things to think about, all at the same time. It was hard enough to remember what to do, let alone to simultaneously co-ordinate the actions. It seemed that I would never get the hang of it. I was getting more hot and bothered, and wondered if I had the energy to trudge back up the hill yet again.

I stood on the hill and then charged down once more. To my surprise, the harness grabbed me by the crotch, for a few brief seconds my feet flailed above the ground before I careered on, grinding to a halt I turned round to see from where I'd come. I was incredulous. I had just flown, even if only briefly! My spirits soared.

With that achievement under my belt, Niki suggested lunch at last. I wiped the sweat from my face, the salt stinging my eyes. We packed up and lurched off in the Moskvich while Niki patiently answered more questions. I couldn't help smiling, proud of my endeavours. I licked my lips, tasting the salt and dust from my exertions.

We found a small restaurant. The food tasted good, especially as I was so hungry. Niki had a dry sense of humour and a way of holding your attention. He described the mystical experience of living in the moment while soaring the skies on your own, free to float where you wanted like a bird on the wing. He described how he would just take off and land on a mountain top, wrap up under his wing and fall asleep looking up at the stars in the clear night sky, on his own in the wilderness, at one with nature and the universe.

After our late lunch we headed to the large landing field used by the novice pilots at the base of the mountain. Niki needed to guide some of the other students on their descent, using the radio. There was no sign of activity at the summit. While we waited he explained the landing procedure, drawing diagrams in the earth with a stick, he outlined the landing field, "You follow the edge of the rectangle – the landing field – taking a right-angle turn when your height is at a 30° angle to the central point of the field, another right-angle turn at 20° and again at 10°." It was a bit over my head, but the reality of solo flying off the mountain now seemed closer.

As we saw the first pilot float off the top, suspended in the air, voices became audible on the radio. Niki introduced himself over the radio and gave an instruction. The pilot responded, like a remote controlled model plane. I was transfixed as I watched each turn the pilot made. The pilot manoeuvred ever closer, following the landing route that Niki had only recently drawn in the dust. He landed gracefully in the centre of the field. I casually wandered over when I recognised a familiar face from the night before.

One by one the others landed safely. "Just wait until you go from the top," I was told repeatedly. Getting off the ground was a feat. I couldn't begin to imagine what it was like leaping from the summit. "Are we going back to the training hill?" I ask tentatively, wanting to fly, but not looking forward to the trudge up the hill.

"Mañana" replied Niki. So I joined the others for a well-earned drink from the bar at the bottom of the chair lift and this relaxed camaraderie continued into the evening.

The next morning I woke up slowly. My blood stirred, but my legs ached, stiff and bruised. I eased myself out of bed and made my way to the breakfast room. There were a group of five sitting at the big table. I greeted them all and listened to the conversation, the discussion was about catching thermals. They could have been speaking another language; this was way over my level!

I studied the faces around the table. A bond held this disparate group together, with a passion for flying as the glue. When you talked to each person individually, each had a different story and background. Something invisible yet very strong held them together. Everyone seemed so close and I felt that I now belonged to this new family.

Back in the Moskvich, we trundled off to the training hill, just Niki and me. The ritual began again. I climbed up the hill until Niki told me to stop, taking my new position; I was now over halfway up the hill. I spread out my wing, did my pre-flight check and readied myself for launch. I was apprehensive as I felt the gentle breeze on my face. I ran through the launch procedure and the words went through my mind, "Are you ready to go?"

I put my best foot forward, the wing inflated behind me and I felt the resistance in the breeze. The wing swung up above me; I glanced up quickly and ran as fast as I could with all my equipment strapped to me. I lifted off the ground for a few brief seconds before touching down gently on the grass. I was overjoyed, carried by the experience of leaving the earth and floating in the air.

I was lulled into a false sense of security and my enthusiasm got the better of me in my rush to progress. There followed a number of aborted launches where I got increasingly frustrated with myself. Eventually I took off, and for a few brief minutes floated off the hill over the patch of grass, and into the ploughed field on the far side, where I landed too fast in the lumpy earth, tripped and twisted my ankle.

In spite of the pain, I was in love again! After dusting myself down and gathering my gear together, I limped back up the hill, inhaling the wafts of camomile rising from the earth. After a few deep breaths to steady myself while spreading my wing on the grass, I repeated the launch ritual and threw myself into the air once again.

Progress was slow and painful, with each launch I moved higher up the hill. The higher I climbed the more I realised that I could seriously hurt myself, and in turn, the more fearful and tense I became. As the sun rose in the clear sky, I stripped down to a T-shirt. I was exhausted by the time we stopped for lunch at a different restaurant.

The warm tasty stew heated me up inside, although weary, my spirits were high. The conversation revolved around dealing with fear, which I had now realised was beginning to hold back my progress. Niki had an enlightened and philosophical approach to teaching people how to fly and I could listen to him for hours.

"When you stretch yourself, pushing the boundaries of where you feel safe, it is perfectly natural to feel fear," Niki expanded. "I started with a fear of heights and keep coming up against new fears as I push against new boundaries of what I believe is possible and what I can do. To go forward, you need to face your fears, which now confront you. In fact, it is pushing through your fear that allows you to grow. Facing fear releases the 'old you' who cannot fly.

Although fear appears so real, it is something that is inside you, an illusion. Fear can grip you like a demon and it takes inner strength to remain still and calm as you stare into your self.

You should ask yourself what do you need to learn because fear will continue to challenge you in many forms. It will keep coming back until you get the lesson."

Learning to fly was symbolic of other aspects of my life I realised. You have a choice when fear raises its ugly head – you can either face it or run away. To face your fears demands courage. It's a trial of nerves; it requires you to reach inside for your inner strength, to stand up and confront the demon inside you. Once you get the learning, you are able to continue on your path.

It would have been easy to find an excuse for not taking my first tandem flight. If I had run away from fear on my first flights on the training hill, I would have missed out on the whole experience of flying; it would have stopped me opening a window to this new world of flight, where fear was only the veil that covered the entrance.

Life is similar; if you consistently avoid or run away from fear you are in danger of becoming a victim. I could blame the events that occurred in my life on someone or something else, like in the break-up of my marriage; I could even say, "It's not my fault and there's nothing I can do". I would be giving away my power, because avoidance diminishes you.

So what if I decide to run away from fear? Demons love to chase you through the labyrinth of your mind, like an over-excited pack of hounds. They smell your fear and follow your scent while you flee. The more you panic, the more they chase – and your fear becomes paralysing and prevents you from experiencing the amazing things that life has to offer – like flying!

So it was my choice about how I dealt with my fear. Would I allow it to torment me or to bring out my inner strength? Would I leave the window closed, or open it? To fly or not to fly, the choice was mine.

Our conversation continued in the car. Eventually my thoughts turned to more mundane matters, I asked about getting a lift to Sofia that evening. "No problem, we'll fix you up," Niki replied.

When we got back to the training hill Niki told me to climb to the top of the hill, while he positioned himself lower down. With my wing behind me, I held the risers in my fingers and gazed out across the fields at the panorama of mountains in the distance. The feelings of fear began in my belly, my mouth felt dry and sticky.

I ran through my pre-flight check, connected with something deep inside me, and committed myself to go. I launched, drove my right foot forward, lifted my wing and ran into the wind. Up I flew, the grass sank below me and I was in the air on my own, where all was calm and still. From the ground, Niki yelled at me to turn to the left; I pulled down shakily on the left control, then hastily on the right. I looked down on the patch of grass before the ploughed field and landed heavily on the ground with a hard thump. That last push through the barrier of fear had been worth every moment of the brief flight, and it went deeper than only flying.

There was time for one more flight, where all I had learnt came together as I consolidated my lessons for the day, and then we were finished. Whew! I collapsed into the Moskvich, feeling as worn and weary as the old car, at the same time amazed at what I had achieved in only three days, starting with the tandem flight on the first day, which now seemed so long ago.

Niki drove us in silence to the small landing field at the base of the mountain right next to the chair lift, a square grass field some hundred metres long, bordered by trees. The landing path was a turn over the tall poplar tree in the far left corner. Behind it stood a monastery with four striped towers.

We approached a number of people to ask for my lift to Sofia, before I was introduced to a guy with an earring in one ear, Nicolas, who was driving a large van with plenty of space. On his T-shirt was written, "I kill people for money. But you are my friend, I kill you for nothing!" He asked me to hang around for some other pilots, who were still flying down, to join us. I offered him a drink, which he accepted.

I watched, mesmerised as the experienced pilots touched down. Some alighted as gently as a butterfly on a flower. Others pulled off daring feats of fast turns close to the ground to impress their audience.

I pulled on the cold beer, my reward for a challenging day. I felt radiant with an internal warmth and gratitude that the gift of flight was now within my grasp. I was elated; this was what I really enjoyed doing.

We packed the large bags containing the wings on the floor at the back of the van, arranging ourselves into comfortable positions on top; there were four of us in the back and others in the seats in the front. With music blaring, we found our way onto the road back to the city, leaving Sopot behind us.

Nestled amongst the wings, I slipped into a reverie assimilating what I had experienced and learnt over the long weekend, drawing the parallels with living my own life.

Like many new undertakings, when you decide to fly, your whole world changes – slowly, at first as you open a window into another dimension, another universe. I was only beginning to realise how the winds of change were blowing through that opening, giving new depth to my experience of living.

I was intrigued and curious about flying, so I had pursued the dream of flight, which took shape until I reached a threshold. That's the point, where I had to decide to make the leap – to go to Sopot and again to jump from the top of the mountain for the tandem flight with Niki. Then each step on the journey became a series of leaps, each step developing inner resources and strength.

Learning to fly is a lesson in getting the most out of your life, initially you will have mishaps, you won't know how to use the tools and equipment and then you struggle with co-ordinating all the things you need to do at the same time. It's important that you don't simply give up, but persevere to achieve the life you want to live.

I had learnt new ways of seeing the world and techniques to launch into the air and land safely. Yet this was just the beginning. Desire, persistence and patience carry you through, as you learn to think and act in new ways. It feels uncomfortable, inside. It pushes you to your limits ... and beyond. It means trusting yourself to make the leap into the unknown.

I was impatient for the next weekend to come, to develop the glimpse of flight I had caught over the last few days.

CHAPTER 4

Early Lessons

*"There's no reality except the one contained within us.
That's why so many people live an unreal life.
They take images outside them for reality
and never allow the world within them
to assert itself."*

Herman Hesse

When you were a kid, do you remember playing a game where you alternately dared each other to do something? The game escalated, where each new dare became more challenging and outrageous than the previous. There was that sense of excitement, of not knowing what was going to happen, as you steeled yourself for your next challenge. That's how flying felt for me, as I waited to find out what my next lesson had in store.

My body ached from the exertions and hard landings from my first weekend of paragliding and the week ahead gave me the chance to recover. I went for a deep tissue massage at the hotel where I had first stayed in Sofia. I winced at the pressure on a particular deep spot in a leg muscle. "Do you feel pain?" asked the masseur. I grunted something in acknowledgement. Back came the reply, "Good, that means you are alive!"

I couldn't wait to go back for my next lesson when I phoned Niki on Thursday about returning to Sopot for the weekend. He gave me a phone number to call, someone who could give me a lift and, one phone call later, it was all arranged.

Early on Saturday morning, we set out along the Stara Planina. The road dropped down into the Valley of the Roses, through the villages and as we drove closer I felt a sense of belonging and familiarity, as though I was on my way home.

We arrived at the clubhouse in Sopot where I saw familiar faces and some new ones. Picking up from where we left off the previous weekend as though it were yesterday, Niki threw me a wing and a harness in the courtyard of the clubhouse. Starting his training that day was a new student, Malcolm, who was slightly older than me. He joined Niki and me in the Moskvich and we cruised through the avenue of walnut trees, past the graveyard on the route to the training hill that I now recognised.

Niki started by getting us to do parachute landing falls on the grass at the base of the hill. There is a knack to keeping your head down and your arms together close to your body while you bend your knees to roll sideways in order to dissipate the momentum of the fall, keeping your arms close to your chest as your hips hit the ground.

My back creaked painfully as I threw myself to the earth and I felt peeved to discover that Malcolm, although older, was much better at this than me. I repeated it again and again until I made a passable demonstration of the fall.

It was time for my first flight so after collecting my gear together, I hiked up to the top of the now familiar hill, inhaling the perfume from the wild herbs, and noticed how the pain from my twisted ankle had now gone.

I psyched myself up on the way, preparing myself for the day ahead.

'Dare to be yourself. It's time to wake up, climb into the driving seat and take control. Draw on your energy, guts and drive that are within to find your true mettle.

Dare to fly. Remember that precious moment when you decide that you're ready. Take a deep inhalation of breath, and on the exhale, just say, 'Let's go!' and launch yourself into the air; then you're away!

Have you got the commitment to throw yourself, body and soul, into leaving the earth? You know you can find technical and logical reasons for not doing it properly, but is your heart in it? In order to fly, you have to get off the ground first. Flying is not an accident. It is a deliberate decision followed through with dedication. You decide.'

Having given myself a pep talk, I found that I was now at the top. It was a clear sunny day and I could feel the heat beginning to build. I spread out my wing across the grass and attached the lines to my harness with the karabiners, ready to fly. As I watched Niki attach a radio to my harness, those familiar feelings of apprehension began to bubble up inside once more. I realised that I needed to start moving, hanging around was not going to help, especially when the conditions were right.

The lessons from last weekend came back to me slowly, especially the parts I had learnt by rote. I prepared myself for launch by running through the ritual of the pre-flight check. I took a deep breath and, on the exhale, I pushed one foot forward and followed the three steps of the launch – inflation, control and accelerate – running headlong down the hill like a wild man. I was off, my feet rose above the ground and once again I was in the air!

Niki stood below me halfway down the hill. I barely had time to think before the instructions came over the radio to turn to the left. I pulled down with my left hand on the control and the wing above me banked to the left. I ran parallel to the hill for a brief moment, and then turned to the right, making an arc through 180°. Turning back through 90° and facing straight ahead into the wind, I dropped to the valley floor. I reached my feet out to gently touch the ground and halt. I felt inspired; my heart and spirit soared.

The lessons continued. Once again I spread my wing at the top of the hill. I became complacent and stopped concentrating properly on what I was doing. A bodged take off dragged me to the right when I didn't take control quickly enough. The wing raced towards the huge holes in the side of the hill while I chased it, determined to get off the ground before falling into the hole. At the last moment, I pulled hard down on my left brake, gained control and turned into the wind. The sense of relief was followed by near panic. I was aiming straight for the vineyard with no time to spare.

I forced the landing onto the grass just short of the barbed wire between the concrete posts that supported the vines. My feet hit the ground hard with a jarring thump, the wing continued, pulling me hard into the wire. It was a crash landing. Everything went still inside while time was suspended. Slowly I came to my senses to assess my situation. Any blood? Any pain? I checked my limbs and body – just a few scratches. It was a close shave.

As I trudged through the wild herbs back up the hill, I reflected on my experience, if flying were a mirror it would reflect back on other facets of my life. What I struggled with in my flying would illuminate other aspects of my life. So if this were true, where did I need to pay attention? What were the links to other dimensions of my life? There should be a parallel.

For example, where else was I being faint-hearted or insensitive? Where else did I need to give my full concentration and dedication? I thought about my daughter, Georgia, was I neglecting her? I felt uncomfortable. What about work, was I being too insensitive? A number of situations over the previous weeks came to mind. The feelings of discomfort amplified within me, providing more than just food for thought. There was a resonance, and it hurt!

So the act of launching became a metaphor, a

symbol for me. By paying attention to what I needed to do for an effective launch, and then taking off successfully, I received a powerful learning. It was a symbol for what I should do in the other dimensions, where flying became my teacher on many different planes. It illuminated my route as I progressed on my journey through life; it ensured that I learnt my lessons, with painful reminders when my attention wandered. My universe tested me. I realised that I had the choice on how to respond, me alone. The choice was mine.

Launching myself again from the top of the hill, a group of pilots showed up in cars and a large van, parking on the grass patch where I usually landed. I left the top of the hill to glide towards my regular landing spot and was transfixed by the van parked right in the middle of my path. It would be a matter of moments before I hit it!

"Look at the empty space," yelled someone below. I shifted my attention to the open grass to the left of the van and the wing followed my focus. I landed safely with a sigh of relief, and it had very nearly been a painful lesson.

A basic rule in flying is that where you direct your attention is where you go. So you focus only on where you want to go and actively avoid looking where you don't want to go. It seems so obvious and yet it still catches me out sometimes, in flying and in life!

I thought I'd learned the lesson well, until the next day when the lesson was repeated. As I came in to land, I flew over a large pool of water from a recent rainstorm. I stared down as I skimmed low above the water, expecting to land gently on the other side. Wrong! I was dumped right into the middle of the pool. My boots disappeared below the water line, into the mud. As my soggy boots squelched out of the pond, it seemed so obvious that I should have focused on the dry earth where I wanted to land, which would have kept my attention away from the water.

You go where you are looking, so you'd better be looking at the right place! If you focus on a tree you are trying to avoid on a landing, you will almost certainly find a way to hit it. Energy flows where your attention goes – it's an important lesson to learn in all aspects of life.

The day's training came to a close. Malcolm was as exhausted as I had been at the end of my first day. We collapsed into the old green Moskvich and Niki drove us to the main landing field to join the others, leaving the bags on the roof of the Moskvich. The air was warm and soft, the wind had died down and the sun lit up the rocks and trees above us. We joined the more experienced students, spreading out on the grass of the landing field, with a drink in one hand.

The discussion drifted to the psychological benefits of flying. Learning to fly is an emotional leap of faith. The experience of free flying is profound; it resonates within you and reveals aspects of your inner self from a different perspective to your usual view. You begin to understand the mental limitations you construct around your life as you jump over the physical and emotional hurdles that everyday life puts in front of you.

When you fly, you are on your own, suspended above the earth, defying gravity. The debate centred on how much you should rely on your instructor. Should you make your own decisions or rely on the instructor to make them for you? You begin with instructions over the radio, then you are on your own and have to take full responsibility in order to survive. That's part of the learning curve.

As the sun slipped behind the mountains, we ambled back across the landing field, up the hill between the old monastery and amphitheatre and onto the upper road leading into town with a view across the valley. In the warm glow of the evening we chatted as we wandered along the cobbled street. Water from deep inside the mountain gushed out of a carved fountain and flowed beside us along the stone gutter on the side of the road. The smell of cow dung filled the air from the animals' journey to their night quarters. It was a timeless scene, made all the more enchanting by the warm air and feelings of physical tiredness and hunger.

In the autumn the year before, at the time when I had first seen the wings on the mountain behind Sofia, my assignment evolved into a new phase. We decided to invest in improving the performance of the sales teams around the country and I volunteered to teach key skills to the front line people. I developed a two-day workshop in sales and communication, which I had tested that August with the team in Veliko Turnovo, the historical capital of the second Bulgarian Empire. The results that followed in that test region drove demand for the training from the other regions; it was time to roll out the sales training across the country.

Two young Bulgarians, Ivanna and Kircho, from the training department were allocated as my translators. Our first meeting was formal, held round a table in the centre of a temporary office near the airport. At first they were unsure how far they could trust me, wary of the foreign consultant with a strange approach to training and development. I outlined the programme, providing them with slides and workbooks in English, which they dutifully translated into Bulgarian. Ivanna was the more experienced and she organised the delegates.

In early November, we started our roadshow, moving from town to town. We held our first workshop in a clapped out old concrete establishment on the outskirts of the country's second city, Plovdiv. The training room was the only one to be modernised in the entire building. Large cracks in the walls of the toilets, allowed you to see right through into the adjoining rooms. It didn't faze anyone; after the collapse of communism and much of the infrastructure in the country, this was a minor indignity.

After everyone had left, we packed up and found our way to the nearest bar, where we poured over the feedback forms, which became a ritual after each seminar. We analysed the results and discussed the implications; Kircho looked despondent. Although the scores were excellent for the overall training, he and Ivanna were rated poorly. A thought came to me, now my challenge was to coach them in their communication and presentation skills by applying the techniques we were teaching our sales teams. They bought into the idea immediately.

We agreed on our new challenge, to do whatever it takes and each seminar to be better than the one before. The roadshow rolled on, in hotel seminar rooms, one town after another. In the bar after each workshop, we analysed the feedback and our own performance. Ivanna's and Kircho's scores improved, becoming better and better after each training, and they pushed me. I had to keep improving my own performance, raising the bar at each workshop. They watched my every move and utterance. In the bar afterwards they bombarded me with questions, referring back to what had happened on the training and what they had learnt previously; they were voracious, devouring everything I gave them. I fast came up against my own limitations. I had a choice, to avoid the demands they were making on me or break through my own barriers. I felt I had to rise to the challenge, and I had to keep doing it, again and again.

We drove ourselves hard. I experienced the reality of the saying 'the teacher learns most'. Moving from town to town, we were constantly together in the car or seminar rooms. We built up our skills and confidence in each other, working seamlessly together. The drinks flowed, we laughed and teased one another, bonding into a close team. By halfway through our tour, we all consistently hit the top scores.

Our roadshow culminated in Varna on the Black Sea in mid December; it was cold, wet and windy. We were exhausted after the final leg of ten days training over the course of eleven days. With the final workshop completed, we packed up, finished our rituals and celebrated the achievement of our goals. I congratulated our team. Finally, we sat quietly in the bar together, waiting for our lift back to Sofia and a long overnight drive ahead of us. Ivanna began to sob quietly, so I put my arm around her shoulders and comforted her, "You must be worn out; the last few weeks have drained all of us, especially you, with the additional hassle of organising all the delegates". She looked up at me, "No, no, you don't understand," and paused, "It's not because I'm tired. I haven't had so much fun for a long, long time and I don't want it to stop." It then struck me how much I had enjoyed myself over the past few months. The full impact caught up with me some months later in March, when I hit the bottom, before my tandem flight with Niki.

Back in Sopot, the symbolism of flying resonated through me. It had a way of illuminating what was happening to me on my journey through life, a voyage of personal discovery. It is so easy to shy away when you reach a barrier, and find reasons for not doing what you would really love to do, for not living the life of your dreams. Even when you can define what you want in some shape or form, it's so easy to find an excuse for not making it happen. Over the years I have found it only too easy to blame others, circumstances, events, childhood etcetera, the list is endless.

Unearthing reasons in the outside world keeps you trapped in your current situation. It means you avoid making the necessary changes within yourself. I had no difficulty in gathering others around me who would agree with me, blaming my limitations on my outside circumstances. With the best of intentions, friends and colleagues at work would condone my response to the problems in the systems, organisation, people or management; and the result would be that I only became more entrenched in my old habits.

I made excuses for not taking the initiative in my life in the past, where I blamed my reluctance to make things happen on the need to earn a living and provide for a family, where in fact I was holding myself back, and in the process short-changed those I loved. It would have been all too easy to have found some trite reason that excused me from learning to fly, perhaps that I was too old – and there I am sure I could have found someone to agree with me!

Finding external reasons is dangerous; it gets you stuck even deeper in the situation, like in a relationship that is not working out well, where you need to change your attitude and behaviour for it to improve. By blaming things on someone else, you prevent yourself from doing anything about it.

Even when learning to fly with an instructor you still need to take responsibility for what happens to you. On one flight, weeks later when I was already leaping from the mountain, I was following directions on the radio from Itso, one of the Skynomad guys. I came in to land, waiting for him to tell me to make the final turn right, into the wind. There was a tree, dead ahead on my flight path, but I was still waiting for the command, which never came, so I had to make an emergency stop. I slammed on the brakes, landing fast and hard, but safely, right in front of the tree. My wing continued; it caught the top of the tree and wrapped itself round the branches. It was painstaking work extracting all the lines and fabric from the branches and twigs without damaging the wing, and then unravelling all the knots.

Itso sauntered over. "What happened?" I asked, "I was waiting for you to tell me to turn." He responded with a smile, "I could see you were safe landing in the tree, which is a pilot's friend, because the branches give you a soft landing. I thought you needed to learn something about making your own decisions. Don't rely on anyone else to make decisions for you. You decide; it's your life!"

In seizing the initiative you take full responsibility for your choices and actions. It means claiming back your power and your life, then keeping it. As I discovered when I leapt from the top of the training hill, there is no room for excuses; it's entirely up to you.

This is not easy to accept; it may challenge some of the foundations on which you build your life. It's not comfortable, when you have to shift your perspective. We all have a fear of the unknown, and you may remember that the change in outlook won't come from outside you, but from within.

If you want to live your dream, the solution is inside you, not outside. I realised that the breakdown of my marriage was caused by me, not getting the work or clients I wanted was caused by me; my problems began inside me, and so did my dreams.

In the past I had drifted in a place where it was

comfortable enough to wallow, and not so uncomfortable that I might actually do something about it. I needed to decide what I really wanted to do. Like a young child, what would rouse me in the morning with a sense of excitement and wonder? Flying had woken me up, what else did I want?

There is an iconic photograph from the Apollo expeditions to the moon, where the Earth, partially lit by the sun, rises from behind the bleached lunar landscape against a backdrop of the dark void of space. Perhaps for many of us, it was the first time we looked back at Mother Earth to appreciate how unique and precious is our planet, how delicate is life. When you look back at yourself, your own inner world, you value the treasures you have within.

To go inside, you accept the existence of an inner world, and in, you venture. As a child, it is easy to go in and out of this inner world, which many adults dismiss as a world of play and fantasy. As you get older, the pressures of society make it more difficult to go back in.

For me the door to this inner world started to close when I went to boarding school from the age of eight. Away from my family for months at a time, my focus was to survive in the unforgiving world of school life. Although I understood the logic and reasons for boarding, I still felt abandoned by those I loved. I avoided looking within and facing the pain of being abandoned, alone in the world. As I grew older I decided to turn my back on this inner world, to shut it out. You may have done something similar. You may even have thrown away the key, after all, it wasn't real – or was it?

What is reality? Your inner world is not real in a way that you can readily share with others, so it's not measurable in a scientific sense. It's subjective and personal; it's how you perceive your universe. It certainly is real in terms of the strength of your feelings – despair, fear, hurt, warmth and exhilaration may all be subjective emotions, but when you physically experience them they feel real enough. And when you feel joy you know you are really living, totally alive!

If this inner world is not objective, does that make it less real? Maybe 'reality' can only ever be perception. The outside world of apparently objective facts is filtered through your senses, which send chemical and electrical impulses through your nervous system, from which you create an internal map of what is in the outside world, an internal construct of what's outside. Therefore, outer and inner worlds are surely both subjective perceptions.

Isn't it curious, that when an event occurs when you are 'down', you perceive it very differently to when you are 'up'? When I have felt vulnerable, a suggestion someone has given me resulted in me feeling that this was proof of my incompetence, and so I resisted picking up their advice and running with it. The same suggestion given to me when I felt confident allowed me to see the opportunity and take it on. My inner state filtered my perception and thus altered how I reacted.

The magic is to accept that your outer reality reflects your inner reality. Then, recognise that you can alter your inner reality at will, depending on your focus – you decide where your attention needs to be and change what you run through your mind. If I am going to present something to a group of people, the response is better when I recall a time in the past when it all went well, instead of one when it didn't!

The power of visualisation works when you imagine your outcomes happening the way you want them to, and taking the action needed. Like making a presentation, the audience can immediately identify when I have a clear idea of the outcome I am aiming for. Where you direct your attention is where you go.

By altering your inner reality, you change the filters through which you perceive the outside. You also change what you project to the outside world, so if you want to make changes to your outside world, as when preparing to make a presentation, you begin by altering your inner world.

In which case, those precious wonderful moments in your life have been created from within you. Similarly, those less enjoyable times are the result of what you have also projected to the outside world from somewhere deep within.

Now, there is no way that I could prove definitively whether this were true or not. What I have found is that it is more empowering to believe that whatever happens to me is my creation. Sometimes events test you when they happen in your world, which do not make you feel comfortable. Leaping off the edge of a mountain tested me, and that was my choice. I didn't want to go to boarding school when I was eight, but if I lived in the middle of nowhere in Africa and wanted an education that was what I needed to do. My father was ready to die and yet it was not easy for him or his family to let nature take its course.

If what you perceive as reality is not in fact reality, but an internal map of an external world, then everything around you has been constructed by your mind. In order to handle the various facets of your life, you have created or borrowed maps over time. Some have been updated and revised. Others may have been formulated a long time ago, and are now outdated. Like using a road map drawn before the advent of modern highways, it can be confusing when you wish to travel from Sofia to Sopot today.

I realise now that when I alternated between my life on the Zambezi and life at boarding school, I operated from different 'maps' of reality, survival and getting what I wanted. When I spoke Portuguese or English, I operated from very different models of reality. And when I confused these maps, I got some very strange responses!

A map may be useful to you, or may not be. If it's not useful, you can change your map, you don't have to soldier on with the same map. You can create a new one that is more helpful to you. You may have more than one map, depending on the perspective you want, after all, they are only models of what's outside.

The ability to play with the various maps requires mental flexibility, discarding some, creating others. In learning to fly, I had to discard some old maps of reality, like dealing with heights, as they inhibited me in the air. From my instructors I learned the language of flying, a new way of thinking and more useful models of reality. You may consider changing maps to be active dreaming. It increases your choices and options, and changes your reality within.

It's easy to allow yourself to be influenced by someone else; we're all moulded by the influences around us – parents, friends, teachers, colleagues, newspapers and magazines, the list is endless. We allow ourselves to be persuaded to do things, to develop our values and beliefs and rarely challenge them. When you start to create what you want, how much of your power do you give away? Do your dreams belong to you, or are they someone else's? The choice is yours.

I sat on the landing field on a warm summers evening and reflected on the clarity of vision that flying was giving me, the stillness of the air adding to the sense of calm. I watched the shadows slowly lengthen across the grass and the last pilots coming in to land.

When I dreamed of flying, for a long time, I had no clear vision. I had a vague notion although I knew I wanted to fly, but didn't know how. I knew I didn't want to take lessons in a small aircraft; I simply craved the freedom of flight. Until the day that wing floated into sight my vision was vague and blurred, and consequently difficult to actualise.

The clearer you make your internal vision, the easier it is for you to achieve it. You need detail; you need to know how you will feel when you are in that imagined situation. Your feelings, emotions and beliefs all contribute to creating a strong vision – and that energy is the catalyst that takes your vision from within and turns it into an outer reality.

When I stood on the mountain of Vitosha and saw the first colourful wing sail into view, my vision crystallised and connected with my gut – in that instant I knew that this was what I had meant when I had announced 'I want to fly.' I could see myself floating through the air and knew that this is what I wanted. The inner vision was as clear as the one my eyes could see – my imagination ran wild and I felt the exhilaration of soaring like a bird. That's all it needed for my unconscious to go to work and ensure that this vision became reality. Holding that – imagining the sense of freedom, how exhilarating it would be to take flight – made that vision become reality. It gave me a clear purpose on which I could take action.

Clarifying your vision helps you to take responsibility for your life to create the outcomes you desire. You have the power; you create your dreams in reality. The choice is yours.

'If I could fly, what else could I do?' The question came out of the blue. Once it entered my consciousness, I couldn't get it out. Round and round it went, working its way inside.

CHAPTER 5

The Leap from the Mountain

"We are not human beings
having a spiritual experience.
We are spiritual beings
having a human experience."
Pierre Teilhard de Chardin

Hristo, a Bulgarian pilot who became a good friend, gave me a lift back to Sofia on Sunday evening. I asked him if he would be returning to Sopot the following weekend, unfortunately not. I didn't want to keep hassling Niki to find who might be making the trip from Sofia and there was no guarantee that I would find a lift. I could have bought a car, but owning a car in Sofia brought further complications, so did arranging lifts for the weekend.

Hristo suggested going by rail and later, during the week, phoned me up with a train timetable. So the next Friday evening at around ten, I made my way to the main railway station in Sofia, to catch the Varna train that stopped in Karlovo, near Sopot. I joined the queue at the office inside the station and in my broken Bulgarian eventually persuaded the weary woman behind the counter to sell me a ticket.

I found the platform and the right train with minutes to spare. I climbed aboard with my overnight bag; there was plenty of space so I found an empty compartment and settled down for the journey. The train may have been old and battered, but it pulled out on time at 10:15 that evening. As the city slipped past my window, my spirits lifted with the sense of adventure of going flying for the weekend.

We left the city lights behind us; the mountains were silhouetted against the twilight sky. I set the alarm on my mobile phone for one o'clock in the morning, just before the train was due in Karlovo. I opened my book to read and after a while I found myself dozing off, nodding to the rhythm of the train, clackety clack, clackety clack, clackety clack. I woke up to the sound of my alarm. I rubbed my eyes and after a while squinted through the window into the darkness outside to see if I could see any lights because we should have been nearing Karlovo by now, and the train kept going. The minutes ticked by and the train continued to clatter along. Eventually it began to loose speed and then slowly screeched to a halt. I grabbed my bag from the rack above the seat. There was no sign of life on the train; everyone appeared to be asleep in darkened compartments. I peered out looking for a sign to tell me where I was, preparing for the struggle to decipher the Cyrillic letters. There were a few lights in the distance; the place looked deserted. At the far end of the train I could see a couple clamber down from their carriage onto the earth by the track. There was no sign in any script, nothing. The station building was too far away.

As I stood in the open door, the train began to move again, slowly gathering speed. It was decision time. I leapt off the train into the dark cold night; I hit the ground and wandered over to the main building. I found a sign; I was in the wrong place; I was in Klisura. I had no idea where Klisura was relative to Karlovo or Sopot, was it before or after? A long time later I discovered that this little town played a key role in the 1876 uprising against Turkish rule, brought to life in Ivan Vasov's book Under the Yoke. I found a bleary eyed Station Master who managed to explain to me that the next train to Karlovo was later in the morning at 06:15. That was five hours away. Shit!

Clasping my overnight bag, I walked towards what appeared to be a cluster of buildings up on the hill. By the drone of the occasional passing car, there seemed to be a main road on the other side of the village. I wondered what to do and eventually decided to hitch a ride. I wandered through the deserted streets, avoiding the drunk who stumbled along the cobbled road towards me.

After a long steep hike I reached the highway and dropped my gear on the grass. Catching the purr of a car speeding towards me in the distance, I stuck out my thumb; it raced past. A long pause followed. I picked up the sound of the next car and had the same reaction; and so the farce repeated itself for an hour. I lay on the grass, resting my head on my kit bag and felt the damp creeping through my clothes.

I considered my predicament. "It's very late. It's dark. You have no idea where you are. You don't speak the language. You can barely read the Cyrillic script. You're getting cold. And there's no way you can sleep here. This is a fine mess you've got yourself into."

I stood up and walked around to keep warm and dry. In the distance there was a drone from another direction, from the village. A large van slowly worked its way up the hill; I stuck out my thumb as it approached and, to my relief, it stopped. I opened the door and asked the driver, "Sopot?" "Da, da," he replied. Yes, he was going to Sopot. I leapt in and smiled at my good fortune. He was delivering newspapers. We trundled along, our laboured conversation punctuated by long silences.

He dropped me off at the main square in Sopot. I made my farewell in my best Bulgarian and holding my bag walked up the hill towards the club. There was no response when I rang the bell. While I waited I studied the front of the building. I reckoned that there might be a way over the top of the door arch. I climbed up the railing, balancing carefully on the tiles, tiptoed along the top, my bag in one hand. Easing my body over the other side, I dropped onto the lid of a metal bin and teetered for a minute, before leaping onto the ground, still clutching my bag.

I tried the door; it was open. I let myself in,

feeling my way round until my eyes adjusted to the darkness; one of the rooms was empty. I undressed quickly and slid between the clean dry sheets with a sense of relief. I lay back and reflected on how quickly circumstances could change, including adversity. All things must pass, and I was just grateful to be warm and dry, to have somewhere to lay my head, before drifting into deep sleep.

It was Saturday morning, when I woke up I could hear voices in the courtyard below, people gathered in the sunshine of the clubhouse to find out about the weather conditions. I pulled myself out of bed, and after breakfast gathered my gear together, expecting to leave the others and drive to the training hill. Niki was busy with pilots seeking his advice; I made my way over to him, and we greeted each other. "So, what do you want to do? Would you like to fly from the mountain now, or later?" he asked.

He caught me by surprise. "Really? Am I ready for this? Wow!" After all the crunches and crashes, he obviously had enough faith in my ability to launch and land safely. I was making progress. This was now the time for my leap from the mountain, solo, on my own, so I must be ready. With great trepidation I loaded my gear onto the roof of the old green Moskvich.

As we were about to drive way, a breathless pilot came running up with his backpack over one shoulder. "Is there room for me?" he begged. Niki looked him in the eye and with a broad smile replied, "My car is like a woman's heart; there is always room for one more!" One more bag was stacked on top of the others and we squeezed up to make room for him. We lurched off to the chair lift.

With a knot in my belly and a smile on my face, I bought my ticket and waited in line. The chairlift didn't wait for anyone; it just kept going. I positioned myself in the path of the chair; my gear was thrown into the seat next to me and the lift scooped me up, to carry me up the mountain.

It was a calm clear sunny morning. The higher up we went, the later the impact of spring. We rode above the trees; it was fresh and green beneath me. Twisting round in my seat, I gazed out, admiring the view of the valley stretched across to the mountains on the far side. I inhaled long deep breaths of the clean fresh air to steady myself. Up, up, up we went.

Before I reached the station at the top, I opened the guardrail, ready to jump off the moving chair. The concrete floor was beneath me now and the chairlift kept moving, I leapt to my left as the attendant whisked off my bag. I hauled the large rucksack with my wing enclosed onto my back and joined the others on the trek up to the launch site. I dared not stare too long at the valley far below me.

We hiked higher up the mountain for ten, fifteen, twenty minutes. The grassy slope unfurled. One by one the others stopped, taking their positions on the mountainside. I found a spot and dropped my gear off my shoulders. I turned around to admire the view. Although struck by the beauty of the panorama in front of me, my heart sank.

I gazed down at the ground far below. The training hill was minute by comparison, a molehill.

"Where is the landing site?" I asked the guy next to me. It was tucked away, hidden from view at the base of the mountain. I was a long way up, nearly a thousand metres above the floor of the valley. I tried to remember three good reasons why I wanted to come here and fly. At that moment it was a struggle to find even one!

My guts churned with butterflies. My mouth was so dry and leathery that my tongue stuck to the roof of my mouth. My heart thumped loudly in my chest. I unpacked, spread my wing, laid out the lines neatly and prepared my gear ready for launch. I approached the more experienced pilot on my right, "How are you doing?" He grunted something to me. "I am shit scared," I confided.

"Don't worry, you're not alone, everyone gets nervous before they launch, you'll be fine," he replied reassuringly, followed with a laugh, "Whatever you do, don't panic!" I closed my eyes and inhaled deeply again in an attempt to calm my nerves.

I returned to my equipment, following the familiar preparation ritual that I learned on the training hill, and reassuring myself that that I only had to do what I had done before on the hill; the only difference was that it was just nearly a kilometre higher! I strapped on my harness, attached the risers making sure they were clear and ran through my pre-flight check several times. All the while my heart beat louder and louder as though it wanted to leap from my chest, I deliberately slowed and deepened each breath to steady myself.

Niki fastened and checked my radio. He rested his hand on my shoulder, looked me over and gave me a knowing smile; it felt like the preparation for some ancient initiation ceremony. In his laid back manner he assured me that all would be well. He stepped back, below and in front of me, to the right. I kept my gaze straight ahead as my knees began to tremble.

"Are you ready, Mike?" he shouted.

" Yes," I choked in reply; I was scared shitless and ready to go! At that moment it felt very strange to be in my body as I prepared to throw myself off the side of a mountain, in the hope of being lifted up by some string and fabric, on a wing and a prayer.

"GO!" he yelled.

I stepped forward firmly with my arms outstretched, clutching the risers in my hands. The light wind filled the wing and pinned me back. I focused only on taking one step at a time. All the training by rote on the hill kicked in automatically, anchored in the memory of my nervous system; I was back in familiar territory. My new instincts took over.

Step 1: Inflation. Up went the wing. I pressed forward, glancing up at the wing, relieved to see it fully inflated above my head.

Step 2: Control. I pulled gently on the control lines, to steady the wing above me, to stop it shooting in front. When I paused for an instant Niki yelled, "Run! Run! Run!" with a rolling R. All the other pilots all joined the chant, urging me to keep running.

Step 3: Accelerate. I charged, driving myself forward and pounded across the grass. Driving one foot in front of the other as the wing pulled against my shoulders, I propelled myself down the side of the mountain.

After a few steps the harness began to lift me. I pushed down on my raised front foot; it never touched the earth. Both feet were now peddling in thin air; the ground was still close. I was up, dangling from the harness by my crotch. I fixed my head dead ahead, my hands were up by my shoulders gripping the control lines for dear life. I hung there not daring to move, frozen in a state of suspended animation. It had all happened so smoothly and quickly.

Over the radio I heard Niki's calm clear voice, "Well done, Mike. You are doing well. Keep going straight out into the valley, away from the mountain." I looked at my hands on the controls; they were shaking, reminding me of my father's when he got very old. Cautiously, I checked the risers and lines. My eyes followed the taut lines to the large colourful canopy stretched above me, all was clear. I was hanging in space, alive. I felt reassured; it had all gone smoothly and all was well.

I wriggled back into the harness easing myself into a more comfortable position. I hung on to the controls watching another pilot ahead of me, in the distance. I followed in his imaginary tracks through the air, straight out.

I steadied myself again by taking long deep slow breaths, while I watched the rocks on the ridges to either side as they fell away beneath me. I drifted away from the mountain, time slowed right down. I wondered how high I was. "Do you dare look below now?" I asked myself "Go on have a look."

Slowly, I moved my head to the left to peek underneath me. Sure enough, the trees and rocks were far below, slipping further away beneath me. I straightened myself and relaxed into the harness, keeping my eyes on the horizon to orientate myself. After the short flights on the training hill, it seemed strange to be up in the air for so long.

A wave of exhilaration washed through me. "You've done it. You're flying! You've left the mountain, you're floating above the rocks, and the trees are a long way down now." I was way up in the air and I had the sense that I was gliding off into outer space, strangely disconnected from the earth below.

A new voice crackled over the radio, giving directions from the landing field. "Hello Mike, this is Orlin. OK, now turn 90° to the left." I pulled tentatively on the left control line, and very slowly I moved left. "Mike, pull harder, stronger." I gathered myself and pulled steadily, more firmly on the left control. I turned more tightly until I judged about 90°.

"That's not 90°, it's only 60°." I yanked harder to the left until I heard Orlin say, "OK. Now turn 180° to the right." I pulled firmly on the right control and sensed myself pivot to the right until I was running parallel with the mountain range. I followed each of Orlin's commands explicitly, trusting in his experience to bring me back safely.

As I listened to the sound of his voice on the radio, I was entranced, gazing at the vista around me, the mountains behind and in front, the villages, fields and forests below.

The Valley of the Roses stretched out to the Sredna Gora mountain range on the far side, merging together in the distance. The clear blue sky was all around me. I was flying in the land of wine and roses.

I was spellbound as though in a dream; I had entered another dimension, a different world. My heartbeats began to slow as I settled down and relaxed into the flow of what I was doing. The breeze was cool and fresh on my face, making a swishing sound as it rushed through the lines. The wind entered the vents in the canopy above, inflating the compartments of the wing, which carried me through the air.

The world looked different from up here, high in the heavens; the magnificence of nature was all around me as I bobbed about all on my own surrounded by empty space. In comparison my usual day-to-day concerns seemed so small and trivial. Flying was everything I expected and hoped for … and more, much more. It was an overwhelming, powerful experience.

The earth came closer as I gradually lost height under the pull of gravity. I continued the manoeuvres above the landing field; I was so engrossed in following the instructions over the radio that I lost track of time.

Orlin guided me through the landing path, tracing the outline of the field, coming to the centre. With a final turn, my feet a couple of metres above the ground, I faced into the wind to touch down pulling hard on the controls to brake my speed. The earth rushed up to greet me. My feet hit the ground running. I kept my balance – just, and came to a halt. The canopy rustled as the wing deflated behind me. I was safely back on terra firma!

My knees shook and a huge grin appeared on my face. Waves of elation flowed through me; a sense of warmth was left in their wake. Orlin wandered over to offer his congratulations, followed by Steve, a Canadian from Vancouver, who had landed before me. My grin got even bigger. The enormity of what I had achieved overwhelmed me. Exhilaration! I was alive!

Steve helped me to fold my wing, giving me tips on how to look after it. When all was packed, I looked around. The world seemed altered now. It felt different; I could fly. I watched someone come in to land. They touched down, and I experienced that wave of exhilaration once more. I threw my kit onto the roof of the Moskvich, an old friend now, and joined the group nearby.

"Was that your first flight?" someone asked. "Yes, it was," I replied proudly. Someone kicked my arse. It was a ritual for the first flight. The new initiate joined the ranks of radiant beings who fly.

We left the Moskvich and the landing field to follow the path towards the chair lift, climbing down a chalky hill through the wood. My head was in the clouds as I relived every moment of the flight. I pinched myself to check if I was dreaming. It felt real enough.

I let my thoughts loose in the metaphor of flying as an analogy for life and everything, a powerful symbol of freeing your spirit. The experience was potent and intense. The question surfaced again, 'So now you can fly, what else can you do?' I vanished back into the memory of recent events.

Entering the dimension of flight was like being born into a new world. You began to understand who you are at deeper levels as you explored. As you experience a series of transitions and new beginnings, death and birth repeat themselves in various forms throughout your life. Each new experience – or birth – is a transformational and creative force.

I reflected back to a birth that I could still remember vividly– that of my daughter, Georgia. Neither of us expected our baby to be born early because we were both often late for everything. It was the summer of 1989; Pru and I went out for dinner together on Friday evening. When we arrived home Pru went straight to bed. A long while later she reappeared and said, "I think it's started."

"What's started?" I asked, confused.

"What we've been waiting for nearly nine months. The contractions!"

I rushed around ineffectually, trying to remember what I was supposed to do. Eventually we made it out the door and I drove us to St Marys Hospital.

The night tide washed a curious assortment of humanity into our London hospital, in sagas that unfolded alongside our own. We hung around Accident & Emergency as the contractions built, in a steady pattern, with long pauses in between. There were tests and measurements. Pru was kept in the hospital into the early hours of the morning. The contractions continued their very slow but steady rhythm. At dawn we were sent home, exhausted after the night's ordeal.

Later that morning we were back, when the contractions reached the right frequency. We were ushered into the maternity room and the midwives bustled about, coming and going. The radio was on in the background with the hourly news bulletins puncturing our reality. Unfolding events in Tiananmen Square in China dominated the news. The Ayatollah had died in Iran. Eastern Europe was restless.

Pru was in agony. I did my best to be supportive, like trying the gas. The birth pains wracked her with increasing frequency. The midwives were wonderful, the High Priestesses of the birthing ritual. They were calming and reassuring. One held Pru's hand while I held her other. The birth unfolded and the baby's head emerged slowly. It seemed endless and enormous. Pru breathed heavily and deeply as she endured the pain.

Once the head emerged, everything happened very quickly. The umbilical cord was wrapped around the baby's neck, which could have been a problem. A doctor and more staff materialised. Everything was all right. The baby was born, a girl! She was tiny and gorgeous, delicate and alive.

The baby was immediately placed on her mother, connected, after an incredible ordeal for both of them. I stared in awe at mother and child. The final rituals were completed. Then it was my turn.

I held the tiny fragile being in my arms, her head cupped in my hand. I gazed into her face. An angel looked back at me, open and trusting. I was unprepared for the wave of love that engulfed me. In that instant, I knew my life had changed forever.

The midwives and nurses left, one by one. We were left alone now in the empty maternity room, just the three of us. Despite the noise of the street outside, inside all was quiet, still and peaceful. These were precious moments, intimate and emotional. We bonded, all three of us. A new life was born. She entered the world and took her place, in her story. She was the true innocent. The adventure of her life was ahead of her, with all its endless possibilities.

"The world is your oyster," I remember my father saying those words to me as we watched the sun set over the Zambezi when I was in my early teens. I recalled those words from Shakespeare again, both when Georgia was born and after I landed on my first solo flight.

Can logic and science ever truly explain the marvel of birth and flight? They both seem impossible; even when you understand the science and technicalities, there is an aspect in both that is nothing short of miraculous. They were moments of massive change and transformation in my life, which opened something inside me of which, a moment earlier, I was totally oblivious, even though I was aware on a logical level of what was going on around me.

Without fanfare or hyperbole, they were moments of pure experience, private and powerful, where I truly felt what it was to just be. Learning to fly in my fifties was a birth into a world of possibility, an initiation that required a leap of faith from a mountaintop.

Free flight seems impossible, but like the metamorphosis of a fat caterpillar into the ethereal beauty of a butterfly floating effortlessly in the air, it's a dream that you can make possible. It's a transformation from within, the death of the old and the birth of the new. Metamorphosis is a magical concept; it's evolution.

By stretching yourself, you expose your limitations and fears, so that you can address them, learn your lessons and progress. The lessons of life are similar; the universe around you presents challenges, which reveal the lessons you need to learn. By having the courage to face these, you can enter the world of flight – into the areas of life you have not yet dared to explore. You can take the leap. Your universe becomes your teacher; you develop and hone your skills, allowing you to evolve into a being that flies.

Flying is a choice. You don't fly by accident, in the same way that you don't run or swim by accident. The choice is yours.

CHAPTER 6

The Cloud

*"To live is the rarest thing in the world.
Most people exist, that is all."*
Oscar Wilde

Like a light to a moth, Sopot had a strong draw on me. I had to come back to fly every weekend, to practise the art of spreading my wings, like a bird preparing to leave the nest. The only way to learn to fly was to launch myself into the air again and again; the more I flew the more I improved.

Each flight was different. Every time I launched there were new lessons to learn. The experience of each flight was layered onto the ones before as I learned to deal with new challenges and changing conditions. I became more flexible and accustomed to use and trust my judgement. Sure, I made mistakes and had to find the lessons in the experience. And then there were those magical flights where I had a flavour of what it was like to dance and play in the air. There were other pilots much better than me at flying, and it didn't matter because the sensation of flying surpassed any comparison with someone else.

You know when you are truly alive – you are aware and live in the moment – it's a feeling that defies description. I would launch into the air and float across the ether with every ounce of my being tuned into flight. My attention turned outwards as I read the terrain, flying over ridges, looking for lift. Any slight movement up or down I began to feel through my harness because you fly by the seat of your pants, quite literally. You make decisions in the moment, every instant you make constant adjustments through shifting your weight and altering the pressure on your controls. In effect you feel your way through the sky.

Sounds drifted up from the world below, blending with my movement through the air. The wind rushed through the lines, connecting me with my canopy above. There was the odd rustle, a partial collapse of my wing perhaps, but by now I'd learned not to panic and make the necessary adjustments to ensure I got back in control and stayed in the air.

The novices who developed the fastest were the ones who were first to leap. They kept their nerve and had the most practice. Some people hovered around, waiting for the others to launch first. When their turn came the conditions may have changed so they might not fly at all that day.

There is an inner game of flying. Launching was an interesting dilemma; it's no place for the faint hearted. If you start the launch half-heartedly or with a shadow of doubt, you probably won't connect. The likely result is you have to abort, or collapse in a tangled web of fabric and lines. You begin to discover that your uncertainty is what holds you back.

You need to commit to taking off and giving your all; anything less is not enough. The pre-flight check procedure is a ritual for you to connect; each step is a strong affirmation. Then when you're complete, you finish with the question "Are you ready to go?"

If your answer is anything less than a resounding 'Yes', then the universe will test you. It's similar to other situations in life where you have had to perform, like stepping up to give a speech, your audience quickly senses how engaged you are.

Imagine what it is like to fly high in the sky. You gaze around at the wilderness, the mountains, rocks, and forests. The craggy ravines lead from the mountain into the plain. Water courses down into the large flat valley with cultivated land, villages and houses, connected by the roads. You keep your eyes peeled for open fields as potential landing sites. Occasionally a bird flies past and around your wing, you may even be honoured by a bird of prey gliding beside you, eye to eye, as you float across the ether together. Is it an omen, a premonition?

The support and friendship of other pilots provided a strong bond. Even though we were alone in the air, a shared passion drew us together. We helped and guided each other, each on their own personal adventure. It was always helpful to be able to talk to someone else about where you were stuck, and what you needed to do about it to break through. It helped to be grateful for all you had been given, including the scary bits that made your blood run cold. There was always more to learn and to appreciate.

You also have to have the gumption to say 'No', and not fly. It requires balance. There is a time to be firm and go, and a time to acquiesce to the elements. An aspect of paragliding is 'para-waiting' – until the conditions are right. You may be risking your life. The elements can be dangerous, particularly for a novice; that's also part of the excitement.

It was a warm Saturday. "Have we got time for one more?" someone asked Niki. We were like a bunch of kids on an outing with an adult. He studied the sky; the clouds were gathering. "Yes, if you're quick." It was a decision he cut too fine, and a lesson for us all.

We leapt onto the chairlift, happy to be squeezing an extra flight in the day. I was feeling pleased with myself, that morning I had learnt to do 'Big Ears', where you pull the lines attached to each tip of the wing, which causes the ends of the wing to collapse. It's a technique you use to lose height quickly. I was in one of the old wings, which was also too big for me; it meant that it was less responsive so I came down and turned more slowly.

We reached the launch site and dumped our bags on the ground. "Get ready and leave quickly. Don't wait, just go," said Niki pushing us faster than normal. The sky was darkening ominously in the distance.

I unpacked as fast as I could and launched behind three others, in rapid succession. The last pilot was behind me and it soon became apparent that I was flying higher than the others in my large old wing.

"Fly away from the mountain, straight out," commanded Niki over the radio. I sensed the urgency in his voice and followed his instructions carefully. "Go to the big field across town by the petrol station, don't go to the normal landing field." We lined up behind each other in the new direction, flying over the patchwork of houses and gardens that looked so small below.

I noticed that I was even higher than the others now, and didn't seem to be losing any height. "Mike, I want you to pull big ears now." I let go of the control lines and wrapped the furthest lines round each hand, pulling down hard, as I had learnt that morning. The wing rustled as the edges collapsed. I looked up to see what was happening, the ends of the wing were folded and flapping. There was a moment of panic, but I steeled myself and got used to it!

Niki instructed everyone to pull big ears. There was a sense of urgency in his voice. The sky was getting very dark over to my right; it did not look good. "Mike, pull down harder." I pulled down as hard as I could, but it didn't make much difference.

"Mike, release and then make the biggest big ears that you can. Put your hands high up the lines first." I let go of the lines and felt a strong lift upwards through the harness, whoosh! I was going up, and fast. I stretched my arms as far as I could, wound the lines round my hands and pulled down firmly. The edges collapsed again, more this time. I watched what was happening with a sense of sickening anticipation. The houses were still very small below and I didn't sense any loss in height. The radio was busy with instructions for the other pilots to lose height and adjust their course; the pilot's name came first, then the instruction. There was a long pause.

"Mike, I may need to teach you spiral turns over the radio," warned Niki.

Spiral turns are used to lose height quickly, especially when a cloud is sucking you up into it. The big dark cloud looming over towards us was a cumulonimbus, an overdeveloped rain cloud, which has enormous upward wind speeds inside. The air expands rapidly inside the cloud, cools and releases the moisture as torrential rain. The air beneath is sucked up into the vacuum created in the cloud. The cloud suck can be so great that the raindrops themselves get sucked back up into the cloud getting larger and fatter. Or get pulled so high into the cloud that they freeze, forming hailstones.

I was much too close to the cloud and was in danger of being drawn up into it. Cumulonimbus is the Great Satan of paragliders – almost certain disaster and death. What happened to Icarus? Was it the sun that melted the wax of his wings? Or did the wind and the clouds pluck out his feathers?

This was as good a time as any to learn spiral turns so I prepared myself for the lesson. The radio was noisy again; Niki and Orlin were talking to each other, checking on each pilot. It seemed that Ricky had landed, he was not answering his radio and nobody could see him.

I looked around with a sense of detachment at the valley stretched below, the panoramic view, and the mountains beyond; behind me to the right there was an ominous rumble of thunder, and blackness. It was a beautiful scene, combined with palpable danger. It seemed unreal; here I hung, suspended in space, waiting for a huge dark cloud to devour me. It was becoming surreal.

"Mike you are doing well, keep pulling down hard, you should be OK like that." I looked down on the small rectangles of gardens and vineyards below. I was not making any headway; in fact, I was moving slowly backwards towards the mountain. I held on tight to my Big Ears and time rolled by. I made slow gradual progress, crabbing away from the mountain. I checked my position. I had now passed the town and was over a large field, heading towards a small lake.

My early lessons from Niki came back to me – always look for at least one possible safe landing site. I decided that it was probably best to land on the other side of the lake. Inching my way over the water, the wind very slowly swung round and I followed its direction. Now well away from the lake, I was above a huge meadow and losing height. Still holding my Big Ears, my arms were getting tired. Someone landed on the grass below, but I moved on past him.

The conditions began to calm now, beneath me was a flock of sheep and goats grazing on the pasture. As I lost height, I gently released the outer lines and placed the control handles back in my hands in preparation for landing. I passed over the animals aiming for a clear patch. A shepherdess gaped up at me, open-mouthed; I passed so low over her that I could see the gaps where she had a few teeth missing.

Easing myself forward in the harness, I pulled down on the controls. I avoided the sheep and goats, and dropped lightly on the field. The wing deflated, and folded neatly behind me. I stood in the field with my feet firmly on the ground, pausing for a moment to appreciate the solidity and warmth of the earth. That was one of my best landings to date!

The shepherdess continued to stare at me with her mouth open as though I had just descended from heaven. I had an urge to give her a papal blessing but settled for a beatific smile instead, mainly in relief at being back firmly on earth. She beamed back at me. Now I felt like an alien from outer space.

A goat tried to chew a corner of my wing; I chased it off and packed up quickly, while telling the radio that I had landed safely. The others were still looking for Ricky. The pilot who I had seen land before me, while I was still in the air, now joined me. After a brief conversation, he left his bag with me and wandered off in search of Ricky.

Moments later he re-appeared, "Ricky is fine, landed safely right by the lake on the other side. It seems his radio went dead! Everyone has landed, everyone's OK."

After waving goodbye to the shepherdess and her flock, we hauled our bags onto our shoulders and walked across the field to the road. A van appeared with Orlin at the wheel and we both jumped in. It was only inside that the full extent of what could have happened began to register.

Back in the club, the drinks flowed and the story was enhanced with each telling as we laughed about what we had been through. It was so easy being bold once the danger had passed, and we all felt so close after our shared experience.

The more experienced pilots were not so flippant, describing the full horrors of the dreaded cumulonimbus and what could have happened to us. From the computer screen, a guy nicknamed 'The Kite' searched the internet and found the story he was looking for, which I read aloud to the others from the screen. It was about a guy in Croatia, Davor Jardas, who described his brush with fate.

It was a hot day. Davor was organising a paragliding competition. The clouds were over-developing so the competition was cancelled. He decided to fly down, before the clouds arrived. He was dressed only in T-shirt and shorts and launched with a few others. The cumulonimbus approached much faster than anticipated. He pulled Big Ears to lose height, to no avail. He did spiral turns in order to lose height even more quickly; it was too late. The cloud suck was too great for him, and into the cloud he went.

You use a variometer (vario) to measure your speed of ascent. The faster you rise, the more rapid the beeps the vario emits. His vario screeched, a high-pitched wail. The water in the cloud drenched him. He knew that he would rapidly get cold and freeze as he was sucked upwards in the expanding air. He had to keep warm, but how? He decided to release his safety reserve parachute, and pulled in his wing to insulate his body.

The reserve hung limply below as he shot upwards. It eventually caught and inflated. He hauled in the canopy, wrapping it around him. He was propelled upwards through the cloud. There was thunder and lightening all around. Frozen, he reappeared at the top, 6'000 metres high. He dropped down the side of the massive cloud until at 3'500 metres he was sucked back in; only to be spat out again at 5'500 metres, he was surprised to be still alive.

He finally lost height unable to control his direction on the reserve. Falling rapidly, he was blown into a forest of dead spiky trees. What a way to go he mused. He crashed into a tree, hitting it with his harness, which broke his fall. He dropped to the ground safely, in one piece, unhurt, alive. The whole ordeal was recorded on his GPS. It was a miracle that he survived unscathed, and still alive.[1]

After the story, the conversation continued, more reflective now. Orlin confided his relief. It was a brush with fate, a baptism of fire, and somehow cleansing - and it also gave me more faith and confidence in the equipment, my abilities and the importance of remaining calm. It was a powerful learning experience.

Niki watched us all, bemused. He caught my eye, "So Mike, do you feel alive?"

"Yes, I certainly do feel alive!" was my response. We both laughed.

[1] The Croatian Survivor, Davor Jardas, www.xcmag.com
(published in Dec-Jan edition) Saturday, 26th July, 1997

A few weeks later, we were at the top of the mountain one morning preparing to launch, Niki came over to me and removed my radio. He told me that my best move would be to fly without a radio or an instructor, to let go of my dependency and to fly on my own; to make my own decisions was the best way for me to progress. I needed to trust myself and build up my confidence.

It gave flying another dimension, a true sense of freedom and faith in your own abilities. On that first truly solo flight, I began to understand how to trust myself more than I had ever allowed in the past. I was struck by the silence once I left the ground. I could do whatever I wanted, when I wanted and go wherever I pleased – and the consequences were for me to live with!

I journeyed down the mountain range pushing my boundaries, and when I didn't make it all the way back home, I had to find a field in which to land. After a long trudge in the heat with my backpack, across open space and dirt tracks, I understood the importance of landing near a road, if I wanted to get back easily.

Flying has an uncanny ability to confront me with my own limitations. I needed to fly through my fears, and overcome my inner demons, and in the process, it somehow raised issues that I was evading, allowing me to deal with them and clear them out, particularly around my personal, work and social relationships.

Flying requires awareness, sensitivity, skill and commitment. It's a dance where you play in the air. It's wonderful when you can transfer this lightness of touch to other aspects of your life where you are required to perform, like persuading and managing people to do something that is important and of great benefit.

Brute force and will power alone do not help you in becoming airborne, or to keep you there. When you try to force your wing to do what you want, against the elements, you struggle and it's hard work. You set yourself up for failure. What is required is a lightness of touch combined with a firmness of resolve.

Similarly in dealing with people, when you try to force someone to do something, no matter how obvious or brilliantly conceived, there is a tendency for them to dig their heels in. You struggle; it becomes personal and it's hard work. You set yourself up for failure.

They both require a sense of elegance, a lightness of touch combined with firmness, in a climate of openness where you can experiment and so allow your true essence to reveal itself. This sets your spirit free so you can soar in the heavens. Flying is elegant.

You have to make decisions all the time and act instantly. You learn to trust yourself, to listen to your intuition, because there is nobody telling you what you should or should not do – and there is no one else you can blame. This creates freedom and responsibility, allowing you to grow and develop from within, which is a rare luxury for many in the modern world.

Sometimes you need a flight that makes you

aware of the dangers that you face and install a sense of respect for nature and the elements. Although it may scare the hell out of you at the time, you come away stronger and wiser – assuming you manage to survive!

CHAPTER 7

An Insight on Flight

"In oneself lies the whole world,
and if you know how to look and learn,
then the door is there and the key is in your hand.
Nobody on earth can give you
either that key or the door to open,
except yourself."
Jiddu Krishnamurti

We were sitting out in the morning sun, waiting to see what happened. The wind conditions wouldn't allow any flying, at least for the morning. A new group of students had arrived late the night before. Orlin gathered them together to discuss what to do, while they waited for the weather to change. He invited me over to join the group. "So, what do you want to talk about," he asked them. The questions flowed, mainly around equipment. So the session centred on choosing the right gear, maintaining it properly and helpful accessories. I found it useful as background information.

At midday some other pilots dropped by to see if anyone wanted to venture up the mountain; I joined them, leaving the new group to practise their ground handling skills, where you practise flying the wing like a kite from the ground. The conditions improved and we managed to fly well into the afternoon.

That evening I joined Justin and a friend, dining together at an open-air restaurant, on the table next to Orlin and his new group of students, who left early for a good night's sleep. Orlin joined us. After thanking him for the morning's session, he confided. "It's not my favourite subject. It's not what I really love to talk about."

"So what do you really love to talk about?" I had to ask.

"How to fly," was his response, and then he opened up.

"Some people learn and understand the theory of flying, the technicalities. They read the books and have a good grasp of the theory. They think they have all the answers. However, they lack the feel for flying. This is typical of many pilots from the West.

"Others learn to fly by trial and error, by teaching themselves and getting a bit of coaching from more experienced pilots. They develop the feel for flying, what they discern through their senses and through their harness. They fly by the seat of their pants. However, they don't have a strong enough understanding of the theory. Many local pilots limit themselves in this way.

"There is a relatively small group who have a

good grip on the theory and a real feel for flying. They're the ones who combine the theory with that feel for flying. There is a genuine integration of these two aspects and they become aware of what is happening at a deep unconscious level. Now they have a profound understanding and they develop mastery.

"For example in a competition, when you focus too much on where you are in relation to the other pilots, you may find yourself slipping back. You get anxious. You start to push yourself. You slip back further. You can find yourself in a vicious circle. The more pressure you put yourself under, the worse you perform. You need to take a different approach.

"You need to let go and stop thinking. Everything you have learnt, all your experience, is a resource that you can access, at an unconscious level. Trust your intuition and fly in the moment – let go. Flying becomes a meditation; it's like yoga, you let yourself go, relax into the stretch and enjoy it. It's not easy to describe what happens, you transcend and go into the flow. You are in the moment, now. You enter another reality seeming to go beyond space and time. Then when you come back and look around, you realise that you are now in the lead.

"It's a matter of trusting yourself and letting go. You still need to learn the theory and techniques. You still need to practise, practise, and practise – so that you can fly by the seat of your pants. You integrate the two; that's what makes the difference. Think of it like a meditation, where you relax and centre yourself. Release yourself from any attachments, be in the moment and go with the flow."

We sat there entranced while Orlin rolled his cigarettes, weaving his experience and wisdom through his words. The warm brown eyes of this gentle giant held ours in turn, captivating us. His love of flying, his craftsmanship, his mastery was mesmerising.

We listened to the master as he drew us into the inner game of flying; it was a personal exploration of what was inside each of us, as a spiritual experience. Your evolution within was the key to your performance in the physical world outside; the one preceded and led the other. Flying was a good frame to work with, as the principles apply to achieving the results you want in other aspects of your life.

And then he was gone. We sat at the table, holding the pearls of wisdom he had given us. We looked at each other, speechless and lost in thought, praying that we would remember it all in the morning.

The conversation slowly picked up again; the drinks flowed and new people came to join our table. We wandered over to a party at Manchova, a traditional Bulgarian wood framed house nearby with a veranda and large patio with a barbecue. We celebrated into the early hours of the morning; it was a clear night and the stars sparkled in the open sky.

In the weeks that followed, I would come back to Sopot most weekends. I sometimes joined Hristo and Zlatimira on the journey from Sofia on Saturday morning. Or else I caught the Friday night train arriving in Karlovo in the early hours of the morning and sharing a taxi into Sopot.

The train journeys gave me plenty of time to reflect on what I was learning as I developed my flying skills. The combination of the emotional charge of anticipation and sense of adventure brought it all to life. My conversations with other pilots and my instructors, particularly Niki and Orlin, allowed me to integrate these practical skills with more abstract concepts. I felt that I was on a journey of self-discovery within, and finding my own path for my life.

"Hi Mike. I read the draft of your book. I liked it, although I think it needs to be deeper," Niki greeted me at the natural water fountain by the chairlift, "Let's talk it through over a glass of rakia at my place this evening." Rakia is the local homemade grappa or schnapps. In the end, we met for a coffee the next morning. The last few months had been intense for him; he had split up with Lena, his partner. He had shared the last few months with a woman suffering from leukaemia, who had recently died. "We talked about what is important in life and love," confided Niki, "It adds a certain poignancy when there is little time left for you to live. I am still trying to understand where my relationship went wrong." We concluded that on one hand there is a pull for freedom, as in flight, and on the other the desire for intimacy and passion; life is played between conflicting forces, and still rests with you.

I realised that the way that I was living my life had veered towards the search for freedom. As I followed this route, I realised that I should dwell on the art of living in the moment, knowing what and how to balance, trusting myself, letting go and finding my flow. It began and ended with me, no one and nothing else; the outside world provided the context and detail to hone my skills.

The path could be scary; sometimes there seemed to be no way out. In the air your wing could collapse, you could be thrown around in the turbulence, trying to break through an inversion in the atmosphere. At launch you could hang around for ages waiting for conditions to improve, then when you launched be dragged up the hill desperately trying to keep control of your wing. Landings could be hard, scraping over the tops of trees when you hit the sinking air. My father's words rang in my ears, "There is a technique to everything." The challenge was to discover the techniques and keep your nerve long enough to apply them – easier said than done!

I kept coming back to the questions of who was I at my core, and what made me who I am, and how could I co-ordinate these aspects of myself to find my way. What follows is what I have found both helpful and useful. Any description can never be completely true as it can only ever be a model of reality. Try it on, and see how it fits; use what works for you and discard what doesn't.

You are body, mind and spirit. Your body is your physical component. There are two aspects of the mind, one of which you are aware, and another of which you are usually unaware – a conscious and an unconscious mind.

You use your conscious mind to think logically, to make decisions. It may be who you consider you are. It is the ego, but it is only an aspect of you; there is more to you than that.

The unconscious mind carries out those functions of which you are not normally aware. It preserves and controls your body; it's what keeps your heart beating and other processes operating in your body. It is the domain of your emotions. It organises all your memories. It is a major resource that you can tap into.

Relatively few people access and use their unconscious mind to their full advantage. Many have discord or conflict between their conscious and unconscious minds. You can harmonise these two minds through breathing and meditation, to resolve internal conflict, which allows you to release hidden power and energy from within.

The breath differentiates the living from the dead. It is also both a conscious and unconscious activity. You raise your energy levels through the breath. It centres you. Notice your breathing now - take a deep breath, and exhale slowly through your nose, lightly catching it at the back of your throat. Repeat a few times and notice how you feel.

Then there is spirit, your higher self. This is your being, your super conscious self. It has many other names. It is your link to the higher realms of creation, accessing resources of knowledge, creativity and power. It is referred to as the connection to universal consciousness, the collective unconscious. It's where we are all connected, as part of a greater whole, as the waves are to the ocean, an expression of man and woman's own perfection, comprising totally balanced male and female energy. Some even deny its existence.

In certain traditions, it is believed that the unconscious mind is the bridge between the conscious mind and the higher self, where the conscious mind has no direct connection to the higher self. The only way for the conscious mind to access the higher self is through the gateway of the unconscious mind.

Meditation is a way to still the mind, to bring harmony to your inner world. By passing your attention through your unconscious mind, you access your higher self, your essential being. It connects and empowers you and is a way to access your inner strength and power. For these reasons, meditation plays a sacred central role in many spiritual traditions.

You are the hero on your journey, which you start as the innocent fool, driven by your optimism and dreams. When I set out on the adventure of learning to fly, I didn't have a clue of where it would lead me. To progress, the fallen innocent becomes an orphan, who leaves the old familiar world behind, and in turn becomes a warrior, developing courage, discipline and skill, which you learn to balance with generosity of spirit.

You set out on your adventure, prepared but not knowing what will unfold, seeking freedom and paradoxically intimacy and commitment. There is an element of risk on your quest, where you confront your demons and pass through the 'death' of the old you. This allows you to create your new reality and in the process you transform and evolve. You realise that your external world is a mirror of what is happening inside you. In flying I needed to push through the barriers of fear within me, learning new skills, to receive the gift of flight. Having pushed through the fear and apprehension, you come out the other side. It is your fear that takes you into the abyss, which is rarely as bad as you imagined. Once you make the decision and take action, the real you kicks in and you find yourself doing things that you had dreamed about.

You return from your journey with your present, now the task is to express and share your newly discovered power, authenticity and freedom. You become the ruler of your new realm, drawing on the power from within you. Your competence is mirrored in the state and prosperity of your kingdom. You close the circle by building on what you have learnt and enjoying the freedom it brings.

For you as the hero, this is your journey in the cycle of your life, where you find meaning to distinguish yourself and evolve. You reconnect in the process to reveal the authentic you, and become whole. You can apply the principles of the hero's journey to your whole life, to a simple project or even telling a story.

I realised that I was following this cycle when I learnt to fly and for each individual lesson. By recognising what was happening at a deeper level within me, it made the experience even richer. The hero's journey repeats itself at increasingly higher levels, like riding a metaphysical thermal, where you are lifted ever upwards.

You have the opportunity to live the story that you want your life to be. So look again at your life with new eyes, be aware of the energy and elements within you. Live and enjoy each moment as it unfolds, spread your wings and fly. Pay attention. No one can do that for you, only you decide. Remain on the ground or soar the heavens; the choice is yours.

CHAPTER 8

Flying with Eagles

"Learning the secret of flight from a bird
was a good deal like learning
the secret of magic from a magician.
After you know what to look for
you see things that you did not notice
when you did not know exactly what to look for."
Orville Wright

Many of our evening discussions over dinner in Sopot touched on the art of riding thermals, rising currents of warm air. Giving you lift, thermals allow you to stay up in the air, and can provide you with hours of freedom. Birds of prey are the true masters of riding the skies, and when it comes to thermals, the eagle reigns supreme.

Thermals are generated by the sun, which heats up the plain and the air on top. The mountain acts as a trigger, releasing the hot air. It's this rising air that creates the cumulus clouds above the mountain. As the warm gas rises, it expands and cools, condensing the moisture into clouds. These clouds are fed by the thermals, which are channels, tubes and even bubbles of rising warm air that are sought keenly by pilots.

Catching thermals is an art form. Each time I entered a thermal I could feel the energy in the movement of my wing. As the others rose and spiralled in the ascending currents of air, somehow, I was left behind at the bottom having to dash down to the field to make an early landing, while the others played around for hours. One Saturday evening sitting on the balcony of a restaurant with a group of pilots, I turned to Hristo to seek his advice.

"The technique," Hristo explained, "is to turn into the side that lifts. When your wing lifts on one side, it's a sign. That's the side that has caught the edge of the thermal. You turn into this channel or bubble of rising air.

"When you feel your ascent accelerate, you circle more tightly into the core of the thermal. You need to feel your way round and imagine that you can 'see' the shape of the thermal. There will be a trigger below - a ridge, rocks or trees - and it may lead up into a cloud. A thermal drifts downwind, so notice where the wind is blowing. Birds and other paragliders may also be riding the same thermal with you, above or below, so notice where they are in relation to you. You just need to imagine it, and then ride it."

I experimented the following day. I realised that my error was to allow the lift on one side to turn me out of the thermal, and what I should do was to turn into the lift; at first it felt counter-intuitive. I practised tuning in to my senses to notice what the air was doing and then reacting quickly to what I sensed. There was certainly a technique to catching and riding a thermal, and it required more practice.

Sunday afternoon, it was late October. I was looking forward to my third flight of the day. I jumped on the chairlift with Alan, who taught English in Sofia. As we were scooped up the mountain, we hung on to our bags, clasping them to our laps, and counted the pilots in the sky as the chairlift carried us up – seventeen, eighteen or even nineteen. They were stacked above each other, rotating together, riding the thermal. The light cumulus clouds were gathered above the mountain, a sure sign of strong thermal activity. Alan told me he was going to be a father and after congratulating him the conversation turned to fatherhood for the rest of the way up.

We reached the top of the mountain. There were four of us preparing for take-off. The guy below me struggled with his wing and aborted, so off I went. There was a soft wind; I made a long run and a wobbly lift off. I felt my way to the east ridge, alert for any turbulence. As I passed above, I sensed a tug on my left riser, which connected the wing to my harness. I turned left to catch the thermal, by shifting my weight on to my left buttock, crossing my right leg over my left knee. I entered the thermal, feeling the lift through my harness.

The wing rocked and rolled, I hung below it and began to swing like a pendulum. I pulled into a tighter turn, warily watching the mountain now I was on the other side of the ridge. I turned right, back the way I came and caught the lift again, this time on my other side. I climbed higher; looking down on the launch site I could see how high I had risen. I leaned into the thermal and spiralled upwards like a corkscrew.

Looking down on the wing below me on the launch site, I watched someone take off. There were two pilots above, who I followed circling up into the heavens. All my senses were turned outwards, tuned into what was happening around me. I looked up at the wing from time to time, checking the movement. My life juices coursed through my veins; I felt alive.

The two pilots above me headed to the east. When I ran out of lift I headed in the opposite direction, over to the west. I felt my way, exploring the air, sometimes sinking, sometimes lifting, and flying over new terrain. This was a new experience for me as I pushed my boundaries and limitations.

There was a brown grassy patch on a ridge, with a lone sheep grazing. It could be the trigger for a thermal so I flew over it. Sure enough, the lifting air caught the right tip of my wing and I applied the techniques that I had been taught, spiralling upwards as best I could. My heart raced with the thrill of the ride. I could feel the activity in my wing as it harnessed the rising air, and I looked up to check what was happening.

An immense eagle appeared above my wing from out of the blue. It was soaring directly over me, wings outstretched. It was massive, seemingly nearly two metres across, and so close that I felt I could touch it. The feathers at the wing tips were extended, each one etched against the sky. The plumage under the wing was clearly defined, including the detail of some white feathers.

I looked around; there was no one but the eagle, now out in front, and me. I thought of my options, "You have a choice. You can stay where you feel safe and comfortable, or you can go with this baby!" There was no way I could turn down an opportunity like this, so I took the leap.

We soared together, gliding through the sky, lifting high into the heavens. We rose upwards; every moment was precious, I felt connected to this heavenly creature, a kindred spirit who led me ever higher.

From the corner of my eye, far to the left, I made out a second eagle, which slid into view, to join the first and glide together, wingtip-to-wingtip. Together they discovered a thermal and spiralled upwards in tandem. Enthralled, I followed into the rising current of warm air. We wove around each other and they slid in and out of my vision as we circled upwards.

The three of us climbed together, as though we were in a dance, where I was a novice. We spun round and round. My right hand pulled down on the control until my arm ached, I pushed my left knee hard over the right to keep my weight on the right side of the harness. The eagles were above me as we rose until we reached the top of the thermal, where the clouds began, known as cloud base. Suddenly it seemed that it was all over; the two eagles floated away, wing-to-wing, across the valley, like two arrows slicing across the sky. They were higher than me and very rapidly left me far behind; there was no way that I could keep up with them. I could only gaze after them in awe and a sense of loss as they shot into the distance.

It was in that moment that I realised how high I was, way up in the air, among the clouds. This was the pinnacle of all my flights. The mountain and valley were stretched out far below; the earth blurred by the haze. I could barely see the other pilots, who were far away now, tiny dots on the horizon. I was really high.

I experienced a pang of anxiety, centred on my solar plexus. A pilot's saying came to mind, "The air is soft. It's the ground that's hard." A smile came to my lips; a twinge remained at my chore, although its form had changed.

On the horizon, two dots floated towards me; I could discern my kindred spirits returning, slowly and effortlessly. I watched the two large birds of prey come closer, glide below me, briefly, together. They vanished into the mountain. I was alone once more. I banked to the left and headed towards the east. Floating high above the mountain range, I played around, floating in the wafts of rising air. There was so much lift on the side of the mountain because the heat was being released from the ground at the end of the day, that it was not easy to come back to earth.

The late afternoon sun cast long shadows across the landing field as I passed over the four striped towers of the monastery and the tall poplar tree. Keeping one eye fixed on the windsock, I banked above the cables of the chair lift, turning again above the trees at the foot of the mountain by the stream. I faced into the wind as my feet reached out to touch the earth, and landed gently; my wing floated to my left and crumpled to the ground, deflating like a concertina. I stood on the landing field, stunned, lost in the silence of the moment, trying to assimilate what had happened.

Over the next few days I was haunted by my flight with the eagles. It was a profound sensation that had now pervaded my life. I felt honoured. My intention had been to learn how to fly; yet this was touching the heavens and flying with the gods.

What had happened? What did it mean? Was it an omen? Judging by the impact this flight had on me, there seemed to be a deeper significance to how these two majestic wild creatures had appeared out of the blue, and unsolicited, had led me in a dance high into the ether to touch the clouds. I was touched and charged by the incident, and felt there was a message I needed to interpret.

Surely it was not an accident. I searched for a deeper meaning and returned to an email sent to me the week before the encounter from Debra, a trainer I had met earlier that year, whose approach was based on ancient spiritual traditions that infuse everything that we do.

"Pay attention to what is going on around you, particularly to animals," was the message from Debra: "The intimate relationship with nature can be experienced by a simple exercise in 'intention'. For one day (or more) ask a question of the universe and set your intention to pay attention to everything the universe offers you.

"As you go through your day, notice even the smallest event. For instance, do you find yourself seeing butterflies or dragonflies? Does the cawing of the crow get your attention? How about your awareness being drawn to certain signs or billboards? Notice what and where your attention goes. Then ask yourself what's the overall message being delivered – how is your question being answered? You can even go so far as to go on the computer and search the meaning of certain animals appearing in your life (search animal totems).

"If, as the quantum physicists and the ancient masters say that the world is more a mass of energy than solid structure and everything is connected, why wouldn't our attention being drawn to the appearance of an owl be significant? We might look at it as a way for our unconscious to communicate with us, utilizing what's available on the outside and bringing it to consciousness." [2]

I searched the internet and read up on the significance of eagles, from Bulgarian folklore to American Indian.

"Eagle medicine is the power of the Great Spirit, the connection to the Divine. It is the ability to live in the realm of spirit, and yet remain connected and balanced within the realm of Earth. Eagle soars and is quick to observe expansiveness within the overall pattern of life. From the heights of the clouds, Eagle is close to the heavens where the Great Spirit dwells"

Jamie Sams and David Carson.

How do you keep one foot in the realm of spirit and the other on the ground? How do you bring your newly acquired experience and skill to the physical? Were these the lessons of mastery?

[2] Debra Fentress: www.debrafentress.com

Desire, persistence and patience should carry you through, as you learn to think and act in new ways. It means letting go of old ways of thinking and acting. It feels uncomfortable, inside, and it pushes you to your limits ... and beyond. It means trusting yourself and realising that you have all you need to succeed. It's not about being perfect; it's being outstanding. Let go and trust in yourself and let the real you shine through. That's what it means to unfold your wings and discover your magnificence.

Once touched, there is no way back. You can revisit, and then you move on. You reconnect to be here in the present, aware of the illusion called reality. You decide to create the reality you want, your waking dream.

I realised that what I missed about Africa was the freedom in the heat, space and wilderness combined with a sense of the exotic. Flying had created this connection within me once more in another plane of existence.

Three of us were packed into the car, our wings folded behind us. We were tired, weary and glowing. Hristo was driving; Zlatimira was in the back, a wing on either side of her, winding her long dark hair above her head. We were returning to the city after spending the weekend flying. We came home to earth, as though waking from a dream.

It was a beautiful Sunday evening in late autumn. The golden rays of the setting sun lit up the mountains around us. It was a magical time and I could feel a warm glow emanate from my heart, at peace with the world.

On the journey back I related my flight with the eagles. When I had finished the story, there was silence for a while, and then Hristo laughed. "I can see Mike turning into a real pilot in front of my eyes," he told Zlatimira.

The sky glowed in the dying rays of the sun. The road unravelled ahead. There was a bond that held us together, invisible and tangible. The gift of flight had been given. The apprentice acquired the art of magic.

Using your newly found skills, you can soar with eagles. Learning to flow with the energy of the elements, you can enter the realm of the gods. Now it was time to come back, to feel your feet on the ground, and experience once again the joy of being alive.

At that moment, a thought flutters into consciousness, "So now you can fly, what else can you do?"

Acknowledgements

There are many people whom I would like to acknowledge in creating this book. Please accept my gratitude and appreciation, even if you are not named directly. I believe that the best way that I can thank you is by passing on the gifts that you have shared with me, allowing others to benefit from your knowledge, experience and wisdom.

My special thanks go to:

My family for their love and generosity of spirit. My parents, Rachel and John, for bringing me into this world, nurturing me and providing an exotic start to my life. Georgia, my daughter, for being an angel. Helen for her love and support. My siblings, Christopher, Jessica, Ros, Nico, Benj and their families.

The flying instructors at Skynomad in Sopot, Bulgaria. Niki, Orlin, Itso, Emo and Fozzy, for your patience and support in teaching me to fly. The many pilots who shared your knowledge and friendship, in particular Hristo and Zlatimira for the discussions, friendship and encouragement over many weekends and evenings in Sopot and Sofia.

The team at BTC. Tony Robinson for inviting me out to Bulgaria. Valeriy Yanakiev, Mira Dumanova and Neycho Velichkov for your support. The training team for your commitment and enthusiasm, putting ideas into practice. In particular Sylviya Andreeva, Ivanna Daneva and Kircho Lazarov, who first planted the seed of writing a book.

The many teachers who have helped me over the years. Leslie Spears for introducing me to the field of personal development and what can be done. David Shephard for training and guidance in Neuro Linguistic Programming (NLP), hypnosis, Time Line Therapy™ and esoterics. Helen Urwin for illuminating the archetypes and the hero's journey. Debra Fentress for your spiritual approach and the lessons of the shamanic masters. Robert Smith for the art of metaphor and mastery.

Lesley Morrissey for helping me to express myself more clearly and painstakingly editing the various drafts of the book. Mamita Woodward and her team at Chimera Design for their creativity on the design of the book and its cover, putting ideas into action and making the book a physical reality.

The many friends I have made over the course of my life in various corners of the globe.

Thank you for your contribution, advice, support, challenges, love, learning, friendship, laughter, generosity, kindness, understanding and bringing me into your life – I stand on the shoulders of giants.

Bibliography

The Art of Paragliding
Dennis Pagen

Thermal Flying
Burkhard Martens

Under the Yoke
Ivan Vazov

Pathways to Bliss
Joseph Campbell

Awakening the Hero Within
Carol S. Pearson

The Hero and the Outlaw
Margaret Mark and Carol S. Pearson

The Archetypes and the Collective Unconscious
C.G.Jung

The Power of Now
Eckhart Tolle

Transcendental Meditation
Jack Forem

Wheels of Life
Anodea Judith

Out of the Blue

Unlimited Power
Anthony Robbins

The Wizard Within
A.M.Krasner

Presenting Magically
Tad James & David Shephard

Time Line Therapy and the Basis of Personality
Tad James & Wyatt Woodsmall

The Secret of Creating Your Future
Tad James

The Holographic Universe
Michael Talbot

The First and Last Freedom
J. Krishnamurti

Peace is Every Step
Thich Nhat Hanh

The Tibetan Book of Living and Dying
Sogyal Rinpoche

The Art of Happiness
HH Dalai Lama & Howard C. Cutler

The Doors of Perception
Aldous Huxley

The Secret Science behind Miracles
Max Freedom Long

The Tarot
Paul Foster Case

The Thursday Night Tarot
Jason C. Lotterhand

Bibliography

The Kybalion
The Three Initiates

Jonathan Livingstone Seagull
Richard Bach

The Way of the Peaceful Warrior
Dan Millman

Zen and the Art of Motorcycle Maintenance
Robert M. Pirsig

Medicine Cards
Jamie Sams & David Carson

The Way of the Shaman
Michael Harner

Spiritwalker
Hank Wesselman

Medicinemaker
Hank Wesselman

The Teachings of Don Juan
Carlos Castaneda

The Road Less Travelled
M. Scott Peck

The God Delusion
Richard Dawkins

The Isaiah Effect
Gregg Braden

Lightning Source UK Ltd.
Milton Keynes UK
28 July 2010

157517UK00001B/4/P